THE AMAZINGLY
ASTONISHING STORY

THE AMAZINGLY ASTONISHING STORY

LUCY GANNON

Seren is the book imprint of
Poetry Wales Press Ltd,
Suite 6, 4 Derwen Road, Bridgend, Wales, CF31 1LH

www.serenbooks.com
facebook.com/SerenBooks
Twitter: @SerenBooks

ISBN: 9781781725986
Ebook: 9781781725993

A CIP record for this title is available from the British Library.

The publisher acknowledges the financial assistance
of the Welsh Books Council.

Printed by Clays.

CONTENTS

I WANT TO WRITE

I want to write

something that will take all I know
        and all I have experienced and all I have dreamed,

and present it to the world,

so that the world says
    "Ahhhh…. *That's* what life is about."

and

    "Now we see."

and

    "That makes sense"

I want to hold out on my open palm, tragedy and love and courage and
cruelty and hope,
        saying

 "Look! Look who you are! This is you. You! You! No wonder God
loves you so."

 And I want the world to see the rich and teeming, chaotic and bleeding

        precious

          perished

            world in my hand

and
recognise the God who made it all,

who loves it all,

who pities and cherishes in equal measure.

I want to write the world,

the world He loves,

And I want the world to see.

To see.

To see.

And when I've done all that, I'll have a bacon sandwich.

Fare thee well Enniskillen, fare thee well for a while,
And all around the borders of Errin's green isle,
And when the war is over we'll return in full bloom,
And you'll all welcome home the Enniskillen Dragoons.

$\qquad$ – Folk song and the Regimental

$\qquad$ March of 5th Inniskilling Dragoons

One night, in a dream, I heard my Daddy singing
to my Mammy.

THE LONDON
PALLADIUM

I love this bit, where the music fills the whole place and the curtains rise and all the stars are on the stage and it's so lovely. The bit where Aunty Nelly usually says 'Come on then, shift yourself – we'll miss the bus again.' because we're at Aunty Polly's, watching her telly and we have to walk halfway across Lancashire to get home. But tonight I'm part of it, on the actual telly, right there in London, me and my amazing talking pony, Sparkle. No, Silver. My amazing talking pony, Silver. A fiery horse with the speed of light, a cloud of dust and a hearty 'Hi hoh, Silver!'

It seems faster when you're on it, the round platform thing, revolving faster than the speed of light, just like Silver, but not up a rocky hillside. Here on the stage. The clapping goes on and on, so that the music is almost drowned out by it and I'm quite hot and it's all a bit messy. I don't want to look at the cameras because, whenever a lady does that, Peter says 'Look at her, gurning. Thinks she's it'. So I look up to one side and Princess Margaret looks down at me and she smiles, with her sticky lipstick smile. I smile back, which is polite, because it would be rude to tell her she's just a clothes horse which Aunty Nelly says. I look up to the other side and there *he* actually is, Cheyenne Bodie in his cowboy hat, half injun, half white man, half American, holding my hand. Cheyenne actual Bodie. And I'm so happy I think I might just start flying, taking great big giant steps through treacle air like you can do sometimes, me, the youngest little girl ever on *Sunday Night at the London Palladium*, and the whole world's waving and clapping, and now they're throwing flowers, and someone leans over and picks me up and I twist around to see and it's only Elvis Presley! Very Elvis Presley. Absolutely Elvis Presley. And he puts me on his shoulders and the crowd is shouting 'Lucy love! Lucy love!' and 'God bless. God bless.' Which they shouldn't. And then Harry Secombe is there and then he's my Dad somehow and my Dad is singing 'Fare thee well, Inniskillen' and everything goes quiet, like snowfall. Just his voice, my Daddy's voice, singing to my Mammy and I know it but I don't know how. And I feel something weird, like I'm being, I don't know..... And now I can smell 4711 which is scent, and I can feel something like a hand touching my hair and something else like a blanket and something else like – oh, bugger.

I'm not the youngest ever. I haven't got a talking pony. I haven't even got an untalking pony. A palomino. Or a dog. Or a fish. I'm in bed. And Mammy is kissing me and I'm that hot and itchy I could cry. It was all so breathtakingly wonderful and right and she only went and ruined it. My Mammy. She's gone now so I try to go back, in my head, to Cheyenne and Elvis and Princess Bloody Margaret who I don't even like. Hasn't even got a crown. Old sticky lips, waving and gurning. Thinks she's it. And I want a wee.

1957 LANCASHIRE

My Mammy came in to tuck me up last night and she wasn't blind. She wasn't even a bit blind. She didn't even limp or anything. She was leaning over me and I was very sleepy and she kissed me, I think. She said something but I was in my dream and I didn't even try to hear her. Then when I woke up this morning I thought, that's funny and I knew it was wonderful and that everything had come right so I sat up, right up and I shouted 'Peter!' He didn't shout back but I could hear him, Peter, over in his room, his and Martin's. I could hear Martin's voice and then Peter's, like wasps, or bees or something. And I knew that all our prayers and rosaries and candles had been answered and Mammy was better. But someone was crying. I had to tell them. Perhaps they didn't know. So I scrambled out of bed which is difficult because it's an Army bed and it crabs across the lino if you don't put your feet down quickly and you can get stuck under Aunty Nelly's big bed. I shouted again, 'Peter! Martin!' But no one answered.

Peter was sitting on Martin's knee on Peter's bed. That's not right. That's not how it is. Peter's thirteen and Dad says he'll hang by his neck one day like a highwayman. Martin's a soldier, on passionate leave, and soldiers never cry. But he was. So I stood for a minute, a second, a breath, trying to understand. I told them 'Mammy came in to me.' and Peter was rubbing his face and he'd gone wet and red and his head had gone small inside his shoulders and he didn't even hear me. Martin looked at me with his wet eyes. And I had a horrible feeling and I knew something without knowing what it was and I had to get my words out quick or everything was going to change for ever. The thing Vonnie Harrison said.

'Mammy came in to me and she's better. I could smell her and she can see.' But Martin just stared and Peter was looking now, and his eyes were little angry piggy eyes and he opened his mouth to shout something but I didn't want to hear so I shouted over him, and my voice was all angry, 'Mammy's better! She came upstairs and she kissed me. And she's not bloody blind, you buggers.' I didn't know I said that, but I did. And before my ears could hear his words which were already coming out of his stupid wet mouth, I ran off down the steep dark stairs and I could hear them behind me, calling, but I didn't care.

I'm clattering away now, bare feet slapping on cold wood, hands on the walls. Bloody Veronica Harrison.

The door at the bottom of the stairs has a hundred coats on it and it swings open heavy, and I see Aunty Nelly Simcock by the fire and she's crying. I say 'Stop it. Don't cry, Mammy's better.' But Aunty Nelly Simcock, who isn't a real aunty, just a half aunty on someone's side, looks at me with her mouth open too and I wonder why everyone has their mouths open and their eyes wet but I know really and I don't want to.

I don't want to know. I mustn't know. Someone shouts 'Shut up, shut up' and it sounds like me. I run past her and she reaches out but I twist away from her big stupid hands and I go into the front hall which is dark and smells of cat pee which Uncle Alf says is damp, and into the parlour where Mammy is and she'll be sitting up, drinking tea with Daddy and laughing, with balloons and everything to celebrate because she's better. And she'll open her arms and she'll say 'Here she is! My lovely lovely girl!' And

I'll throw myself into her arms and everything will be mended. It will. It will. It will.

Mammy is in her bed and she's on her special pillow and she's sleeping. Daddy is beside her and Aunty Nelly Bourne has her hand on his shoulder and it's all wrong. All my happiness and knowing is just there, ready to break into a million pieces if I let it, if I let them, if I can't get the words out. The magic words that are true. And if I can't stop their words which are wrong and not true.

Aunty Nelly and Daddy are turning to look at me, but Mammy isn't. And I'm prickle eyes and tight fists, so angry because they're going to ruin everything. I just know it. Daddy takes a breath and the words are right there on his tongue. I knew something wonderful and now it's like custard in my brain and the world has slowed down and I could kill someone. Everything was mended and now they're going to say something and it won't be any more so I shout at them, before they can break it all, 'She's better! My Mammy's better!' And Dad says 'Come here, love.' And Aunty Nelly moves towards me and I look at Mammy but she doesn't look at me and I shimmy away from Aunty Nelly and I start to climb up onto Mammy but the sheet's too slippy and she hasn't got a blanket. She should have a blanket. And Aunty Nelly puts a hand on me but Dad says 'It's alright. She can't hurt her.' And it's true. I can't hurt her. She can't feel me. Even when I dig my fingers into her arm and shout at her, into her face 'Mammy!' she can't see me.

Vonnie Harrison said she was dying and so did a man ages ago but I called Vonnie a big stupid liar and now she was right and I'm the big stupid liar.

I stop trying to climb into her arms, and my pyjama trousers go up my bum and it's all so wrong I can't even begin to put it right so I don't care about my bum or my cold feet or Mammy's head turning towards me at last but not smiling. Her mouth open. I slide back onto the floor and all the breath goes out of me and I just feel sad like the whole world is sad and all of it, it's all in me. We just stand there, sit there, lie there and we none of us move. Then I put my hand on hers and she doesn't squeeze and I know then for good and for ever this is how it is, it's so wrong it can never be right again.

I say to Daddy 'She was better. She came in and kissed me.' and Aunty Nelly starts crying.

1958 LANCASHIRE

No one knows what a fusilier is, or what a CSM is or anything. Dad says when he comes back to Golborne it's like the war never happened. I tell Joe Grimshaw that fusiliers have hackles and that a hackle is the feathers on a soldier's beret but he puffs his cheeks out and blows a fart on his trumpet and Aunty Nelly shouts up through the scullery roof, so we laugh. I live with my Aunty and Uncle because my Mammy's dead but he lives with his Dad and a fancy woman because his Mum's in Winwick Asylum with her mad brain. The fancy woman's called Peggy and she kisses Joe and calls him 'Sugarplum' and he pretends he doesn't like it. His Dad's a foreman up the Sunpat factory, and he's always lived here in Legh Street, even when I was going to Egypt and Cyprus and all over with the Army. Vonnie next door says Army Brat and Dad says it's something to be proud of. So I am.

Mammy was so proud she made Dad sing to her, the night she died, 'Fare Thee Well Enniskillen' because she's trailed through all the war zones in all the world with the bloody Inniskilling Fusiliers. That's what she said and Dad always said 'don't exaggerate and it was only Scotland and Egypt and Cyprus and Ulster and Scarborough' and then they'd both started laughing and so would we. Ages ago. When we were alive.

I've been left behind for a bit, but it won't be long so I keep quiet and wait for everything to go back to how it was, only in Heaven and for ever, with mammy, my mam. If I don't say anything. That's what I think.

I should stop doing marching and going on about the Army and the IRA, because now I'm in civvy street like everyone else. That's what Uncle Alf says, but what does he know, he's never even been in the Army. He was in the mines in the war while my Daddy was at Dunkirk, fighting the Germans and getting an ulcer with all the spam. It was ages ago, years before I was even born, but when he had a cold last Christmas he said he caught it standing in water for bloody hours at Dunkirk and Aunty Nelly laughed. I didn't. It's no laughing matter. And anyway, Martin's in the Military Police so that makes me a soldier's daughter and a soldier's sister as well, so up yours, Vonnie Bumface.

Joe was sitting right here, where we're sitting now, on the scullery roof, practising his trumpet when he fell through. That was weeks ago. Absolutely perfectly where we are right now. He broke his ankle but he could've broken his damn neck if the wash tub hadn't been full so he had a soft wet landing. For a soft wet lad, Aunty Nelly said. I like Joe. He's twelve and he has big thick glasses and smiles and he says lightning never strikes twice so he's pulled me up to sit with him on the mended bit while I wait for Dad. He's doing Cherry Blossom Pink and I've got my fingers in my ears and he's trying not to laugh because it breaks the noise. I've drawn a dog on his leg plaster and he says it's quite like a pony and shows talent.

Dad's got a day's leave, and he's coming to see us so I'm watching out for him when he walks past the wall by the paper shop. Handsome is as handsome does and Aunty Nelly says my Dad is both.

Fare thee well, Enniskillen, fare thee well for a while
And all around the borders of Errin's green isle

And when the war is over we'll return in full bloom
And you'll all welcome home the Enniskillen dragoon.

Dad sang it just like Harry Secombe when Mam was dying, but I didn't hear because I was in bed and so was Peter. He says they should have woken him up but Martin says he has to stop thinking that, because it's mad and what would he have done? Peter says he'd have said goodbye and he's right, so Martin doesn't say anything, just looks sad and sorry. Aunty Nelly says everyone cried and then Mammy said 'My big brave lad' and that was about Martin, and then she said 'My thorn between roses' and that was Peter but we're not to tell him that, and then she said 'And Lucy. What'll happen to little Lucy?' and then she gave up the ghost. Like Nelson in that painting, only in bed, and she didn't have an eye patch. Or medals. She was just Mammy in a bed with a dunloppilo pillow, which is lovely for her poor head.

When I die I want someone to sing to me, but not that song. I'll have 'Lay Down Your Arms' which we used to sing in Omagh, walking down the lane, Mammy being the Sergeant and me and Thomas from up the road being the British Infantry.

Come to the station
Jump from the train
March at the double
Down lover's lane

My brain's sad now and the trumpet's full of spit and stuff so Joe's cleaning it with his shirt bottom, and I'd like to stop thinking of dying but I can't so I decide to think about Heaven instead and I go like Saint Theresa, gentle and pious, looking up at the sky with a smile. I think maybe if you think the right things you'll get a halo like in the paintings. Joe says what's wrong, am I sick or something and I say shut your face.

Then in the glen
Where the roses entwine
Lay down your arms –

He's here! I see his hackle when he turns the corner at the bottom of the hill and it's like I'm back home, with the Army, and all my friends, and all the Army mums and the soldier dads and my heart lurches happy and I jump down and scrape my bum but only a little bit and I swear the bugger word and Joe laughs again and I'm off, running to meet Daddy. I shout 'Peter! Peter! He's here!' But I don't know where Peter is and I'm running faster than the wind and I can feel my elbows up near my ears, like a Greek athlete, and Daddy's getting bigger and I can see the khaki of his uniform and I can feel it scratchy and itchy and lovely even before I get there and then I hear his shiny boots on the road ringing out like gunshots and I shout Dad! And he laughs and then I see her. A lady.

She's as beautiful as Grace Kelly, who isn't Grace Kelly any more but Princess Grace. And she's a bit like the pictures of the Queen. Not the crown and all that, just her face. And her hair when she sits side-salad for the guards outside Buckingham Palace on the biscuit tin. She's wearing this lovely sky blue skirt and jacket and Aunty Nelly takes one look at her and slams into the kitchen. Her name is Norah and she's the most beautiful person ever probably. One of them. I can't think of anything to say. Dad shows her Kitty Lob, who's fast asleep by the fire and when he touches her ear she rolls onto her back and stretches, yawning a perfect pink yawn and Norah laughs a lovely laugh. I tell her that when Aunty

Nelly got Kitty Lob, years ago, a little girl lived next door and she would try to call her, 'Kitty, love! Kitty, love!' But she couldn't say it properly so Kitty became Kitty Lob and Norah says 'How delightful!' And when my Daddy puts his arm around her, I can see, absolutely see, that they are Madly In Love.

Peter comes in and Dad says 'Ah, my second born!' and Peter starts to grin but then he sees Norah and he says 'Who the hell's that?' Aunty Nelly comes out of the kitchen and she's been crying but everyone pretends she hasn't and Dad's handing round sandwiches and Norah takes her gloves off and says 'How lovely.' If she was in blue down to her feet and a towel over her head like the statues, she'd be the Virgin Mary but when I say this to Dad he laughs and Norah nudges him, quite hard. Peter's leaning in the doorway and Daddy's told him three times to come in properly for God's sake, but he just stares back, like you're not supposed to. Aunty Nelly's going on about how it's hardly a year since Mammy died and Dad's gone tight and fierce and when he says 'Fourteen months' Norah puts her hand on his arm and it all goes quiet, badly quiet. She's going to go off on one, is Aunty Nelly, and when she goes off on one Uncle Alf goes to the pub and then she cries. And the night is always bad. She's already full of tears and her voice has gone scratchy and she's trembling. So I clench my fists and concentrate, think of something, think of something. And then I do.

I make a noise and everyone turns to look at me. I jump up and run into the yard. He's in the old enamel tub in the corner, in the shade. Nitzi the Natzi.

Norah frowns as she looks in the jam jar and there's this lovely whiff of Apple Blossom. Which I know it is because I can see the little bottle in her handbag. Crocodile skin. Aunty Nelly has Violent Water and Mammy had stuff for her forehead called 4711 when the headaches started that killed her, but this is what the BVM smells like only it's wrong to call her that. The Blessed Virgin Mary. Father Liam said 'Hasn't she suffered enough without you being a smart alec about her, Lucy Gannon?' Aunty Nelly jumps when she sees the jar and she starts to say 'Get that bloody thing out of my kitchen' like she always does but she only gets to 'Get that-' when Norah says 'A newt! How sweet.' and smiles her lovely smile.

And then I know, just know, for certain and for ever, that everything is going to be alright. Nitzi the Natzi looks at her. Frankie Arnold says newts give you warts but not if they only look at you, and anyway that's frogs. I tell Norah that he's getting a new name, like Princess Grace. He's not Nitzi the Natzi any more, he's Norah, after her, because she's beautiful. Peter laughs but it's not a happy laugh. Aunty Nelly gets up and nearly knocks the teapot over and goes into the back, and she says to the mangle 'And so it bloody starts' and Peter turns like a sentry and goes out into the back yard and two of the coats fall off the door he slams it so hard. Daddy says, very loud and cheerful, rubbing his hands together even when it's not cold at all, 'I know, Lucy Lastic, let's go for a walk, show your Aunt Norah the sights.' So we leave Aunty Nelly crashing and walloping in the scullery, and I walk between the handsome prince and the beautiful princess and there are rainbows and butterflies, with bluebirds dropping rose petals on the path in front of us all the way up Legh Street and past the peanut butter factory.

My sweetheart is a soldier
As handsome as can be

I wish everyone was out to see us, lining the road like they did for the Queen Mother in Scarborough that time. Dad says there's not much to see in Golborne, but there's loads. When we get to the stream Dad says that the name Golborne means stream where marsh marigolds grow and Norah says 'Or old prams and mattresses' and we all laugh.

They're going to be married. I think for a minute that I'm going to be the bridesmaid which I was once, in Cyprus, when a bloody old Eoka man called me bad names in Greek and Dad said take no notice unless they've got a grenade in one hand and the pin in the other, which he hadn't. But now he says that Peter and me can't come to the wedding because of school and the house move and all that. Dad having to move from Chester to Warminster which is the length of the country and never the twain shall meet. Martin is going to be there, because he's got leave specially, and he'll be there for Peter and me as well as for himself. Like we're there with him but we're not. I don't know how that works but Dad gets a bit cross and says it just does. They'll save us some cake and they'll be busy getting a new home ready down there in Warminster, and my new bedroom. Dad will come back for us in just a few weeks and that's when the story will really start.

I wonder what this is, if it's not the story. Maybe it's someone else's story, or maybe it's Aunty Nelly's, not mine and Daddy's which is still on page one. But what does that mean for Mammy who never lived long enough to be in this story at all? Maybe she was in a different story. Dad says 'You're very quiet.' and Norah says it's a lot to take in.

Before they go, Norah shakes Aunty Nelly's hand and they smile big smiles and they are very very nice to each other. Aunty Nelly says that I like to sing myself to sleep and Norah says that's not a problem, I can sing my little heart out. Which I don't want to, really. And Aunty Nelly says that I'm my mother's image and that Mammy used to sing too, and it gives me comfort. Norah says again, sort of slowly, and the smile looks a bit different now, that it's no problem, she understands, and I can sing myself to sleep every night.

No one knows where Peter's gone and Dad says he'll be back and it'll take time and Nelly says 'Aye, it'll take time, and there's no rush'. And everyone smiles and nods and I say 'What will?' but no one says.

When they've gone, arm in arm, Harry Secombe and Princess Grace, walking away down the street to the bus and then to the train and then to Daddy's regiment and then to the church where they're going to be married, I hop into the yard, and if I put my foot down they'll miss their train and Dad won't get her to the church in time which is one of his best songs, so I don't put even a toe down. Aunty Nelly's sitting on the step, with her big knees wide apart like Mr Chop The Butcher in Happy Families and she pats one fat leg and I flop onto it and we sit there, not saying anything for ages, Aunty Nelly stroking my hair, and breathing funny. My head is so full of so many words that I can't pull any of them out at all but after a long time I say that Norah talks like the wireless and Aunty Nelly says she's got marbles in her gob, but I know that's not true because I saw her gold fillings. Gold. That's how rich she is. Princess Grace of Morocco rich, which is where they wear fezzes and Daddy has one of those, brought back from Egypt, where I had a swing and we had a dog, left by a sergeant who'd gone back to England.

Kitty Lob comes to sit on Aunty Nelly's other knee and we both stroke her, till she starts lashing her tail and sinks her teeth into my hand gentle and slow, with her eyes rolling. Aunty Nelly says 'You bugger' and shoves her off and she stalks away, murderous. Kitty Lob, not Aunty Nelly.

There's a little altar to Mammy in Aunty Nelly's bedroom, only you have to call it a shrine because only pagans do altars to dead people. Anyway, there's a photo of Mammy, who is Aunty Nelly's sister, and a photo of me when I was new born with Mammy and Daddy, and a plastic flower and a Mass card and a candle. Sometimes there's a cowslip or a buttercup by the candle and I wonder how it got there. I know Aunty Nelly put it there really, but I like wondering. It's like fairies and Father Christmas, it isn't true but it ought to be. And the world would be a better place if it was. That's what Aunty Polly says.

On the floor, next to my bed, which Daddy told Norah is only fit for a toddler, but it isn't, so there, there's another photograph of Mammy and new born me. If I stare at it for a long time I can make myself cry. So sometimes I do, and it makes me so hot I get a headache. Uncle Alf said 'Well, stop bloody looking at it then.' But I can't. It's all there is left of Mary, my Mary. Daddy read a poem at the funeral but that's all I can remember from it. And the chocolate biscuits. They weren't at the funeral they were at the wake when everyone was being so nice I thought maybe I was dying too and they didn't know how to tell me. Shirley East says people die all the time. Every time you breathe someone dies so sometimes I try not to breathe but it's very hard and I keep thinking of the people dying. I try not to think about what happens when I sneeze or cough, whole bloody families wiped out.

Peter came back just like Daddy said, but he won't talk to me and he told Aunty Nelly that he won't go to any bloody house with that cow and Aunty Nelly didn't even tell him off.

Imagine if you sneezed and that was a granny gone and a mammy and three children and a dog. Even if no one knew it was you, imagine.

The shrine's a bit dusty with Aunty Nelly's talcum powder so I give it a quick wipe with my sleeve as I tell Mammy about Norah. I'd like to light the candle but Aunty Nelly said if I do that again I'll need a bowl under my arse to catch my teeth and who's going to give us another house when this one's burnt down? So I don't. I get into my nightie and squeeze my hands together really tight so I can feel sweat between them and screw my eyes up, and bow my head like on a First Holy Communion Card and I say three Hail Marys to Mary and an Our Father to Jesus the Son of God. And I say thank you for Aunty Nelly not going out tonight. And it's only when I'm in bed that I remember about Purgatory and if you can't even pray for your own mother in the agony of the flames it's a poor do. I want to get out and kneel down and do a PS but the bed is warm and the lino's cold and my head is full of Norah and the new house I'm going to live in, and the new Mummy I'm going to have. Not a Mammy. A Mummy. A beautiful Princess Mummy.

Fare thee well, Enniskillen, fare thee well for a while
And all around the borders of Errin's green isle
And when the war is over we'll return in full bloom
And you'll all welcome home the Enniskillen dragoon.

THE NEXT DAY

When I open my eyes, it's morning and Aunty Nelly says we have to tell the teachers we'll only be there another month. So it was all real. Not a dream. Peter doesn't say anything and when he goes like this he's ugly so I tell him and he says he'd rather be ugly than a thick little silly bitch who has her Mammy crying in Heaven. Aunty Nelly slaps him and I don't get what he's on about and she says it doesn't matter, Peter's just being Peter. And Peter says 'Mammy's looking down on us, crying because you've forgotten her.' And I say she's not bloody looking down anyway because she's bloody blind, so there, and Aunty Nelly slaps him again, and then me, and now we're all crying.

The teachers say they'll miss me and when Father David comes for Catechism I tell him about Daddy getting married and he says it's like a true romance story and better than a filum. He always says filum because he's from Mayo, which is a wild and woolly place and full of little people. I don't know why. Father David is very fat but he's still a priest and Aunty Nelly calls him Father Tuck and Uncle Alf calls him Father the F word. He ties his cassock around his big belly and plays football in the yard and broke a window once and Miss Foster tried to tell him off but they both started laughing and Miss Foster walked away, with her hand stuffed in her mouth and Father David wiped his eyes and said 'Ohh, dear, oooh, dear.' All smiley.

I've saved a pound and I pay for a Mass for Mammy's soul,

and I ask Father David to say it. Fat or no fat, says Aunty Nelly, he does a grand Mass. When he lifts the host his voice goes wobbly with the miracle of it and if I squint I can nearly see Jesus where the little white wafer is. If I wasn't a girl I'd be an altar boy. I can't see Jesus at all when Father Byrne gallops through the consecration so fast it all sounds one long word with the bells making no sense and the missal pages flying in the pews like a load of pigeons set out from a cage, as everyone tries to keep up. If I couldn't be an altar boy, I'd be a golden retriever which are beautiful, with sad eyes. Or a pony with eyelashes.

I try to tell everyone how beautiful Norah is, but they didn't see her and I run out of words. I can't believe not even one of them saw her when she was there for a whole afternoon. And then I remember that when the Queen Mother came to Scarborough and everyone lined the streets, me and Mammy were waiting bloody hours and there was no Queen Mum and no Queen Mum and no Queen Mum, and then I needed a wee but I'd already held it in for ages and I couldn't hold it in any more and just as everyone was leaning into the road, at last, and there was a sort of rumble of happiness from the crowd, and down the street they started waving their flags and shouting, I had to tug on Mammy's arm, crossing my legs and dancing, 'I can't wait. I can't.' And Mammy looked bloody murderous and her teeth were together even when she was talking and she yanked me off to behind the hedge. And when we came back the Queen Mum had gone and everyone said she'd been a sea of blue. Remembering is good, and bad. The bad bit is Mammy talking through her teeth, and knowing that I ruined it all but the good bit is the two of us laughing on the way home and Mammy wiping her eyes and saying 'Maybe she caught a glimpse of your bum.' And maybe she did. Daddy said that made me 'By Royal Appointment' which is not at all like going to the dentist but something they write on syrup tins, next to the lion.

And I do the thinking in my head and I add up that it's days and days since Uncle Alf did it. And I think maybe it's finished now. Somehow I know that it's finished now because we're going to live with my Daddy but I don't know how I know it. And I'm still not absolutely sure it's finished because when Nellie goes round to Theresa's on Friday Uncle Alf sends Peter out so I sit very very still like always and I wait and I pray and this time it works, the prayer. Uncle Alf reads the paper and after a bit, when it's all cold and quiet he looks at me and he doesn't put the paper down like always. He's very still and I'm very still and I wonder what will happen but I sort of almost know it won't be the thing. Then he says, strangely, 'You don't want to be sent back, do you?' and I don't know what to say, what is the right thing to say, so I just sit still like he says to. And then he says 'They'll send you back if you say owt. You know that, do you?' I nod my head and I want to cry but I don't. And he says 'Well? Do you want them to send you back?' and I know I have to say something. And my voice is very scratchey and I say 'I won't say owt.' After a bit he says 'And?' and I say 'I'm sorry.' And he nods and says 'Get out my sight, then.' And I sideways past him and out the door and my heart is banging but I run up the jitty, fast as I can. And that's the end.

We catch the bus into Wigan on the last Golborne Saturday and I get new shoes and a new coat even though Easter was ages ago. Peter gets a new mac and because he's fourteen years old Aunty Nelly gives him a pound to go to the market and find some long trousers. He comes back with the trousers and five Woodbines. I saw the packet and when I started to say something he did a snarl, so I didn't say anything after all.

On the last Golborne Sunday Father David talks about us from the pulpit, how we're going to start a new life with Daddy and our step mother and that makes me think of Cinderella and Snow White who both had stepmothers. Maybe not Snow White but Cinderella definitely did. Everyone looks at us, which is not nice, and then they clap us, which is something you shouldn't do in church because it's not a music hall for God's sake, and Aunty Nelly says Father David is just asking for trouble and it'll be half naked girls with feathers doing the can-can next.

When Dad comes to collect us, I'm waiting with a suitcase, a bag, Rita doll, Polly doll, Teddy and my scooter. He says bloody hell and pulls a face at Aunty Nelly but they're not really talking although they pretend they are. He's come in a taxi which is like a funeral car but there's numbers on the side and a thing dangling. A rabbit's foot. Someone's eaten the rest of it. I try to give Kitty Lob a quick kiss but she doesn't want to know, and I get in the back with the dolls and Teddy, and Peter gets in the other side but he only has a bag so there's just room. Uncle Alf puts an arm out to me but I get in the car deadly quick and Aunty Nelly pokes her head in the door and gives me a rough kiss, like she's angry but I know she isn't. She did lots of them when Mammy died. So I wave all the way down Legh Street while Peter looks out of his window all hunched up. Then we're at the station and getting onto the train and Daddy gives up trying to talk to Peter and says 'A new life, eh, Lucy Lastic?' And I'm so happy I can't speak, not even when the scooter keeps catching me hard on my shin where Dad's carrying it and the bag in just one hand.

The train seats are a bit itchy but I don't say anything. Going away, going away, that's what they say, the wheels, not the seats. And when we go over the wee rough bits they say 'Lucy Lastic! Lucy Lastic!' and it's all absolutely glorious like in the hymns and I think of people escaping from prison and soldiers running into the sea at Dunkirk, and birds in the sky and all of us free.

That makes me think of Uncle Alf so I think of something else, quick, but my brain is empty and I don't know what to think about instead. Anything will do.

We're quiet for a bit, staring out of the windows and pretending we're really interested in the streets and the shops and the houses and then the fields. Daddy starts telling us all about the new house and about Warminster which is the School of Infantry. I already know that this isn't really a school at all, but just something they say. Peter sighs, noisy, and folds his arms. Daddy pretends not to see and says that he's the Company Sergeant Major in the pay office but we already know that too. Everyone knows that but his voice is lovely rumbling and it makes my head tingle, so I don't say 'I know' which Aunty Nelly says is enough to drive a saint demented.

He's been a CSM ever since I was little and we lived in Cyprus with EOKA and then Egypt with Nasser and Scarborough where I got lost and they thought I'd fallen off the cliffs into the sea and the police came but I was only sulking in the garden, asleep. That was when Mammy said I'd be the death of her but I wasn't because that was something else. I thought it was a conker in her head but it wasn't, it was something they couldn't take out and you could have taken a conker out I think. So, it's a pity it wasn't. And she was only joking anyway and she said I was a case. And we were in Bloody Ulster before Mammy died and that's where the Catholics threw stones at me because Daddy's a soldier – and the Protties threw stones at me because I'm Catholic. I used to run across the swing bridge with all the bloody Catholics in the world on one side and all the bloody Protestants in the world on the other, all of them throwing stones. Bloody Omagh. I hope all the houses fall down and everyone dies. Martin went to a Brothers school where they caned you but no one threw stones at him, so he joined the Army before they called him up. And we all got nits, even Martin who was home on passionate leave, and Mammy, who couldn't see by then, cried and Daddy slammed a door so hard the house shook. Sometimes it's like Daddy's forgotten we lived together all those years before Mammy died.

I don't know why I'm so angry.

When Mammy was in hospital that first time, in Bloody Omagh, and she was with all the old people because she was Catholic and the Prottie hospital wouldn't have her, I had to sit outside the ward waiting for Peter to come out before I could go in. And a man in a brown overall stopped and said 'Are you the soldier's bastard?' And I was only seven or six or something so I didn't know I wasn't a bastard and I said 'Yes' and he said 'I hope your mother dies in agony' and he walked away. That was the first time I knew Mammy was dying and I couldn't breathe or think but Peter came out and said I could go in, so I went in. I wanted to throw myself down and scream and kick and hit my face, but I didn't. I just climbed on Mammy's bed and got told off and looked all through her locker and found some chocolate which stuck in my throat because my mouth had no water in it but I knew I mustn't cry because we mustn't upset Mammy. And when I think of that man I want to kill him. I want him to die in terrible agony. I want to slice him open and pull his sweetmeats out and burn them in front of his open eyes and say to him 'My Mammy, my Mammy, my Mammy.' So he'll remember and know why I'm doing it. That what he said and how he said it and how he just walked away, that was a hurt worse than the nuns in the Congo with their breasts chopped off. My Mammy.

The look that man gave me and me only a little girl.

The big fat Catholic fucker. One day I will find that man and I will kill him over and over again till the end of time.

I can feel my heart beating and that means I have to think of something else, before it explodes like Mary Harrison's granny did, and they had to burn her new sofa and cover the stain on the carpet with a rug. Mary let us go in to look at the stain but then they moved house and when we asked the new people, who are Scottish, could we go in and look at the blood they told us to piss off. I don't think they're Catholics.

To stop my heart banging, I float up to a cloud and I'm looking down and the train is like a wee caterpillar on the railway track and I can see me in a window and I look happy and everything's lovely. I can't see Peter but that's no loss. I'm going to live happily ever after, so I am. In a lump of the country Daddy says is beautiful. I say 'Like the Black Hills of Dakota, like in the song?' and he says 'Better.' Dad says we'll live on a ranch and I can have my own pony. He's joking about the pony.

Let me be by myself in the evenin' breeze
And listen to the murmur of the cottonwool trees

The train is rocking gently and the fields are slipping past and after a bit my eyes start closing. My hand is in my pocket, around a cigarette card Frankie Arnold gave me, Elvis Presley in a white jacket with pearls on. And as my eyes close Elvis comes to sit beside me, across the seat from Daddy, and even with my eyes closed I know he's watching my reflection in the window, which is a good thing to know, and he smiles at me when I wake up with a jump and can't remember where I am. Elvis smiling, not Daddy. He's doing the crossword. Daddy, not Elvis. Dreams are like real sometimes and sometimes real is like dreams. When we get off the train in London I'm all crumpled and hot, and a little bit frightened but I don't know why and Daddy takes my hand and the scooter hits me behind my knees and he says sorry and I pretend I didn't feel it and there's a big swoop in my belly like I'm going to be sick and I want Mammy and Auntie Nelly. One or the other. Or both.

London station is full of smoke and smell and pigeons and a long long way from Golborne. And Dakota. Roll on Warminster. Peter looks small in this big place and I think he's just Peter really, not this furious person I don't know. Inside the furious person, there's still a bit of Peter. I touch his hand but he pulls away and turns his back.

There's another train. And for the first time when I think it would be nice to see Elvis again, he just is there because I've thought it. So I must have brought him with my thinking. Like rubbing the magic lamp. And then I try Mario Lanza and there he is, and his suit's a little bit too small just like on Aunty Polly's telly, and he's very smiley, with smooth hair. The two of them, liking me and me liking them and it's grand. And in the middle of 'Be My Love' the train stops and Daddy wakes me up although I'm awake already. We're there. Here. 'The bloody South'.

WARMINSTER

The house is red and big and on Station Road in Warminster, right next to the police station, so Daddy says if we ever get lost all we have to do is follow a policeman. I'm a bit sad that we're not in the married quarters with the rest of the Army but Daddy says this is much better as it's a hiring. I've never lived in a hiring before. I think it may be something to do with Norah looking like the Queen. Maybe she's related. We were always in MQ's with Mammy and once in a Nissen Hut which we hated at first but then loved because my Aunty Betty lived next door. Not my proper Aunty Betty but someone I called Aunty Betty, with a mole on her nose and she used to swim in the sea in her knickers and bra. She had twin boys and them and Peter were blood brothers and the bleeding bit on their wrists where they mixed their blood with mud and feathers all went bad and they had to have poultices. Anyway, it's a very nice hiring and I'll get used to it.

My new bedroom is a dream. Lilac. Peter's is bigger but white. Norah leaves us to get settled in and changed so I open Uncle Alf's wartime suitcase which Aunty Nelly said is a disgrace but he's not made of money. I look at all the clothes and wonder which ones. I call across the landing to Peter but he closes his door so I put Rita Doll and Polly Doll on the pillow and choose something special which is last year's Easter skirt with the pleats, and then sit on the bed with Teddy, wondering where my scooter is.

There's a picture on the wall, Mary and the baby Jesus and he's all dimples and puffy little arms and legs and a double chin. I can see his thing, like a teapot spout, short and stout. They can't do you for saying that because it's true. And Mary's a bit soppy, like Wendy Matheson. I make the sign of the cross just in case but things that slip out are only half sins. It's the thoughts you think and stay thinking about that are the proper sins.

I can hear Daddy and Norah downstairs, the rumble of him and the softness of her. Although the room is lilac the curtains are pale lemon. Norah said she'll find some better ones but there's nothing wrong with them. There's a crucifix over the bed and a shelf for my books but I haven't got any. Norah said 'Really?' Like it was an incredible thing, like dragons. Or being invisible. Aunty Nelly only had one book, *Dr Dolittle*, and I read it so many times I full-blooded hate it now, with its silly snub nosed drawings and the stupid push-me pull-you. My old bedroom had piles and piles of knitting patterns, tied with string, and boxes of old shoes, and all Uncle Alf's bowling stuff and trousers that didn't fit him anymore piled on a shelf and they'd fall on the bed in the middle of the night, which was annoying but now, sitting here, I wish I had a few knitting patterns, so I could make up a family with them. A smiling family, a Dad with a pipe and a boy with a model Spitfire, a girl with a paintbrush and a Mam with a mixing bowl and a pinny and all of them with Brylcreem hair. I wonder if I should go downstairs but just as I think I should, Daddy calls up, 'dinner in five minutes, you two' so that's a relief.

I make a bit of an effort and get dolled up. Hair ribbon and necklace. The ribbon's a bit long and my hair's a bit short so I do a big bow like 'On The Good Ship Lollipop'. Norah looks at me, smiley and then sort of blinks and she looks at Daddy and he says 'She dines on fresh cokey-nuts and fish f-rom the sea.' And then they say I look lovely. Which I did feel but which I don't feel now.

Peter comes in and sits down and Dad says 'For God's sake, Peter, crack a smile.'

She dines on just cokey-nuts
and fish f-rom the sea
A rose in her hair, a gleam in her eyes
And love in her heart for me

Tea is hot. It's proper dinner, with roast potatoes and gravy. Dad winks at me and says 'Celebration' and it's just lovely. Then Norah takes the knife out of my hand and puts it back sort of sideways and turns my fingers on the fork so that my wrist's flat and gently nudges my elbow off the table and she smiles but it isn't a smile. You should chew everything twenty-five times, which I didn't know. Daddy winks at me again and says I'll soon be a lady. I should drink a glass of water before every meal because then I won't eat so much and that won't do me any harm at all. That's Norah again. Peter says 'Can't we just eat the damn stuff?' And I think Dad's going to slap him but he doesn't, he just says manners maketh man and I say I don't eat my peas off a knife and Dad gets the joke but Norah doesn't and I tell her the 'I eat my peas with honey' poem and Norah looks at Peter and then at me and then at Dad and says it's not going to be easy, is it?

I can't sleep. It's only half past seven. Aunty Nelly would be having a glass of something now and I'd be colouring in. Or drawing a pony. Half past bloody seven. Norah says every hour before midnight is worth two after it but I didn't know anyone had to pay for them anyway. Peter's reading a book on his bed but they said he could sit with them and he said 'No' and Dad gave him a hard look and Peter got tears in his eyes and I felt sorry for him because, I don't know why. But I did.

And there are lots of things that make this a glad place to be. I think of the brick path in the back yard and Uncle Alf's arm and the smell of him, and I'm glad.

Norah unpacked my things, shaking everything out like she was angry and folding some of them up again and shoving them into an old bag. I thought she said it was for the jungle and that was funny but it's just her lovely voice and she actually said for the jumble. And she found the picture of Mammy with me new born and she went a bit slow and put it next to the bed so now I'm staring into it, into Mammy's eyes as she looks at the camera, waiting for the moment when Mammy speaks. She will, one day. I saw this filum at the convent in Bloody Omagh, where there was this big crucifix in this old attic and a little boy was crying and Jesus came down off the cross and held him, tight tight and said kind things. Jesus coming down is better than nothing right enough, but if Mammy could come out of the frame that would be much better. Mind, then she'd be a little Mammy small enough to put in your pocket which is no good anyway because she couldn't grab you and pull you into her and make fart noises in your neck and nibble your ears and kiss you and kiss you and kiss you, laughing. That's what would be good. Not bloody old Jesus. Which slipped out so it's not even a venial sin or if it is it's a very small one. And now my pillow is all wet and I can't bloody breathe. I had Mammy's pillow once but I haven't got it now. I want the smell of her so bad my chest hurts. Then it goes a bit easier and I say a decade of the rosary for the repose of the soul of Mary, my mother, which I have to explain because there are hundreds of Marys in the world, and I say it in my head like the Pope, all Italian. I don't know where my Rosary is so I have to count the Hail Marys and I keep forgetting how many I got to, so I sing Faith Of Our Fathers quite quietly to make up for any gaps. And

I'm doing that hiccup crying thing and I hate that.

And then it's morning and even though I brushed my teeth last night I have to brush them again! I tell Norah that I've not eaten anything at all in the night, but she puts the toothbrush in my hand and says 'Back and sides, up-down and round' and there's a load of blood in the basin which is very worrying but Norah says it's because I've not cleaned them properly before. Which I have. The cheek of her. When Norah's gone downstairs I look in the mirror. The little girl is dying and it's absolutely tragic to a grand degree. All the doctors gather round and stare down at her, worried. The head doctor, who looks like Perry Como, says 'This child is a hopeless case of TB of the teeth and she must have whatever she wants, whatever her heart desires.' I start thinking about what I would ask for if I could have anything in the whole world and I've just got to a palomino pony and a guinea pig when Daddy shouts up the stairs 'Have you gone and died up there?' And it just slips out, I shout back 'Any minute now.'

I try to open Peter's door but there's something in the way and just when I'm trying to shove it open he suddenly yanks it and there he is, all angry and I say 'Stop looking like that.' And he says 'I will if you stop fucking breathing.' And he goes downstairs in front of me, clattery, which is aggravating because I was ready first.

The F word. I don't tell on him.

SOMETHING WONDERFUL

There are too many new things to think about. They make me dizzy, all the new clothes and shoes and things to learn and do and the new school and the lilac walls. I've tried really hard not to, but I don't quite like lilac. And the church is the same but different, there are different priests but they say the same things and there's the same smell to it and my head gets all mixed up and I think Mammy was here in her coffin and then I remember that she wasn't but I keep thinking that she was. When I remember the funeral I remember it here, not there, where it was. Which is very aggravating and people think I'm lying about having a dead Mammy and I shout at this boy and tell him to shut his buggering face. I tell the dinner lady that Max Bygraves is my Uncle and the lady frowns and says 'But he's a Londoner and you're from the north, aren't you?' And I say so is Uncle Max. From Liverpool, he is, and he was going to marry Mammy but Dad got there first. I don't know why I say that. I keep saying things and it's like nothing's real so everything could be, and no one knows me so I could be anyone, and nothing matters anyway. There's something big and cold and hurting in my chest and I want to shout it out but I can't, so I shout other stuff instead.

And the next day I walk all the way home for lunch but when I walk in Norah stares at me and I know I must have done something terrible again, like not liking the lovely fish she cooked with the slimy skin. We look at the clock together, which explains things to Norah. It isn't lunch time but only playtime and Norah walks me all the way back to the school saying it's an easy mistake and everyone must have done it at some time, which is kind of her, but not true. The teacher whispers to her about me shouting at that divvy boy and some other things and at tea, which is dinner, Norah tells Dad that I've been buggering and blinding all over the place, willy-nilly. Daddy looks sad and when I explain that I think maybe my brain has gone he says I have to stop thinking about things and just get on with it. I tell him that I can't turn my brain off because I've tried with the people dying every time I sneeze, but anyway, I don't want to because it's my Mammy, isn't it and no one can stop me thinking about her anyway. I keep shouting 'anyway' and I'm not sure what I started saying before it turned into something quite rude and it's the first time I've answered back. And Norah looks at Daddy and raises her eyebrows like she's really surprised but she isn't, she's something else and I don't know what.

I don't know why I'm so angry.

Peter's at a different school for big boys but he says he's not stopping there. He says he's going back to Golborne and Dad says Aunty Nelly doesn't want him, which I think isn't true, it's Uncle Alf who doesn't want him. And then Peter says right, he'll join the bloody Navy and I ask is that the same as the Merchant Navy and even though it was a joke Dad tells me to stop being a little clever dick and Peter smiles for the first time in weeks. I think I may properly hate Peter.

That night in bed, I'm not a bit sleepy and I'm on my second hymn, 'Mater Amabalis, Ora Pronobis', all about the Star of the Sea which is another name for the BVM and I've just got to 'pray for thy children who call upon thee' when the door slams open and Norah is there, her eyes bright and her voice wobbly, and I

41

have to stop that damn howling and get to sleep, for pity's sake. When she's gone, Peter opens his bedroom door and he looks at me across the landing and he laughs. Not a nice laugh. I get out of bed and slam my door and then he slams his and Dad shouts up the stairs 'Bloody hell. Get to bloody sleep, both of you.'

There's things wrong with me that Norah says need sorting and we go to the doctors just about every week. I have to jump up on the table and the doctor draws a curtain and Norah stands holding her handbag, looking the other way. I like the doctor, and he winks at me when he says his hands are cold and then he gives me a Quality Street from a big jar and I'm allowed to root around for the toffee one. I think all doctors have Quality Street. That's how rich they are. Norah doesn't look at me at all and on the way home she holds my arm just above my elbow, not my hand, and she doesn't talk. I think she's annoyed but I didn't do anything.

A few days later at dinner, which is tea, Daddy says he has something wonderful to tell us. We're going to have a sister or a brother. And Norah pats her belly. Peter goes very still so Norah talks to me. I'm going to be a big sister so we have five months to get me sorted out, because I want to be someone a little baby can look up to, don't I? Someone who knows, Norah says, staring at my mouth, how to eat like a lady not a navvy. So I chew slower, counting to twenty five, and when Dad asks 'Boy or girl, what do you think?' I swallow first then say 'One of each, please' and it was the right thing to say. We all laugh and Norah stops staring at my mouth. Then I take a big breath and decide not to think about it and jump right in like Dad says I always do, and I say 'Can I call you Mummy?' And everyone's happy. Except Peter.

I'm not very happy, but I am quite happy, and I know that I'm very lucky indeed and that this house is bigger than Aunty Nelly's and bigger than all the other married quarters we've lived in, and that I'm being taught how to be a lady, and that I was turning into a little savage up there in Golborne. And soon I will be a big sister and I will have a little baby to hold and to love. So I am quite happy, and I've landed on my feet. Like a cat.

It's my birthday on December 8th so we have a cake and Aunty Nelly sends a *Girls' Crystal* annual which is out for Christmas so I'm lucky because I get it before everyone else. Dad and Mummy give me lots of things which are very nice, a notebook and a smart biro, socks and knickers. Peter comes in to me that night and sits on the side of my bed and I remember the morning when Mammy had died and I feel sick and think maybe Aunty Nelly has died. And he's not angry like usual and he talks to me which is strange and should be lovely but it's not, because he's got a funny voice and I think he's going to cry and I really don't want to cry, not on my birthday. He says Norah's told Dad that he needs discipline and Dad says she's right so he's joined the Navy right enough and after Christmas, very right after Christmas, he'll be off to HMS Ganges which not a ship at all, but a big building where all the boys climb a mast and wear bell bottomed trousers. He says 'I can't stand it here, Luce' and suddenly I do want to cry and he grabs me, and squeezes me and mutters into my neck, not my ear 'We'll be alright.' And then he won't let go and he's crying and he keeps saying 'I'm sorry, Luce. I'm sorry. I'm sorry.' I know why he's sorry so we just sit for a bit and then he pushes me away but gentle, and he wipes his face and he says 'Least that's all over, eh?' and it's almost like we've talked about it and I just nod. I'm glad he said it. I used to think I wasn't real, and it wasn't real, or it was the devil, or he was the devil and no one else knew, or I was the devil so no one must ever know, but I always knew deep down that Peter knew, and now I knew for sure. So that was good.

A rose in her hair,
a gleam in her eyes
And love in her heart for me

Anyway, anyway, Christmas is going to be a magic time, like Bing Crosby and that Danny Kaye film. I hope it snows but Daddy says it won't. We have a TV now so if I was allowed I could stay up and watch the Palladium on a Sunday, without walking all the way across Golborne in the rain to Aunty Polly's, but I have to be in bed so I don't ever see it although when everyone talks about it at school I pretend I have. Peter's packed his bag and he unpacks it every day and then packs it up again. And now that he's going he manages to talk to Norah and she even talks to him and Dad laughs a lot and pats him on the back, but I wish he wasn't going. Martin is in Ulster with the Military Police and Peter will be in Portsmouth with his bell bottomed trousers, Aunty Nelly is in Lancashire, Mammy is nowhere and I have a lilac bloody bedroom.

Mummy is huge and when she comes downstairs Dad sings 'Mighty as a Gannon one' and she has to sit down to peel the potatoes. Dad says it's not Gannon one, it's gallon one, which is a ship. There's a Christmas tree in the front room which is called the sitting room now and when I first see it it's so beautiful I would quite like to cry but then Dad says 'Better than all the other Christmas trees eh?' But I can't remember any other Christmas trees so I say 'No.' And he says 'Better than all the other Christmases, eh?' I can't remember any other Christmases but I know Mammy was in them, so I say 'No.' When we go to the boating lake he says 'Better than Wigan, eh?' but I can only think about Aunty Nelly so I say no. When we walk in the fields he says 'Better than Golborne Hollows, eh?'. I always say 'No.'

I do remember one Christmas. When Mammy was in the front room dying and Nelly was working in the off licence, and Peter was asleep, and I don't know where Daddy was. Uncle Alf woke me up when it was dark and took me downstairs and he opened all the Christmas presents, and it was horrible. I was crying and Nelly came in and she was angry and Uncle Alf pushed me off his lap and I sort of fell but no one helped me up. She kept saying 'My sister in the next room!' and he kept saying 'One fucking beer' and she pushed me up the stairs and I couldn't breathe I was crying so hard. Peter was on the landing and when I got to the top he just went back to bed, but I couldn't stop crying all night. In the morning all the presents were wrapped up again and everyone pretended they were all a surprise. I don't know why. That was the start I think.

Last week Mum took me to the doctor again and the doctor looked at her funny and said something about something, an ostrich or something, and she stood up really quick and held my arm and said 'We're going home' and we went out, without saying goodbye or anything. That night she said something to Daddy but I didn't quite know what she said and they both looked at me, and then Daddy looked away and said 'Let it lie, then.' but after that Daddy stopped looking at me, and I don't understand. I don't want to, either. It's like the picture of Jesus bleeding blood in Gethsemane: I don't want to look at it because it won't help.

Aunty Nelly sends a doll with her own dummy, all wrapped in green paper with gold bells on it and Mummy says I'm too old for that sort of thing and Dad gives me a set of Alice books, in Wonderland and somewhere else, but I don't like the pictures so I'm only going to pretend to read them. Aunty Nelly sends Peter five pounds and Dad gives him ten. It's all lovely because Mummy's knitting little cardigans and being all dreamy and Dad's painting the baby's room and he's never painted anywhere before and they laugh all the time. Mummy sleeps for two hours every afternoon and I draw ponies to send to Aunty Nelly or watch Children's Hour or read a book from the help-yourself pile at church. Mummy checked the first one but Dad said 'if you can't trust the church, who can you trust?' So now every week no one checks what I put in the bag I keep my missal in. Sometimes it's Georgette Heyer and all about history and young handsome captains, and sometimes it's about gangsters in America who say things that are quite hard to understand. On Christmas Eve I'm halfway through a story about Philip Marlowe when the priest comes for his Christmas money and he asks how old I am and when I can't remember Dad makes a face because I'm so stupid and says just turned nine, though you wouldn't know, and the priest makes a hump sound. Daddy says as long as it's not *Lolita*. I'll keep an eye open for *Lolita* next week.

There's extra sums to be done all through the holiday, not homework, extra ones no one else has, because I've barely got the understanding of a six year old. Mrs Marshall says it's cause for concern but not yet alarm. I sit at the dining table and stare at the sums until the page goes blurred, and Cliff Richard and Bobby Vee, who is American, come to sit opposite, and they stare at the sums too and Cliff says they're not easy and Bobby says 'Gee, they're stinkers.' which makes me feel better. I can't do them and I can't do them. Dad says God help me when they get to long division if I can't add bloody thirteen and sixteen and eight. But I can't see why they make it so difficult. We could just forget numbers and no one would miss them. Peter says if I had twice as much brain I'd be a half wit, but then he laughs, right in my face and says I don't even understand the joke. Which is true.

Two is like a swan and four reminds me of D so that might help.

Apart from the sums, Christmas is going to be lovely. I'm going to remember it for ever, even with my bad brain. For the first time I go to Midnight Mass and it's so holy and cosy, with everyone smiling and all the men smelling like dad's whisky and his pipe, that I look up at Mummy and whisper 'I love you' which is the first time I've said it and she gets tears in her eyes and afterwards, on the way home, walking through the wet streets, she says to Dad 'I feel so guilty' and Dad says 'Give it time'. They're talking about the turkey which is going to take eight hours at regular something. Then she says 'Three's perfect and four's.....' But she makes a little laugh sort of noise and says she's sorry and Daddy doesn't say anything. I pretend to be busy hopping over the pavement cracks and they both look at me. After a minute he puts an arm around her and he says this is how it is and she says she knows. I don't want to think about it. There are some things you don't want to think about. Christmas is the happiest time of the year.

In the morning it's funny because it feels like Sunday but we've already been to Mass, so we have breakfast which is bacon and eggs which we never have usually. Then we go into the sitting room and we take it in turns to open our presents. Peter has some really boring things he needs for the Navy like soap and toothpaste and he says thank you really nicely. I get a jigsaw and a picture of a snowy field with ponies running across it. I don't know why. I think maybe they've been frightened by something we can't see, just outside the frame. Mummy says we can hang it in my room and I say 'Lovely. Thank you.' But she looks a little bit as if I should say something else and I don't know what it is. Then there are brown parcels to open and they're from Martin, in Belfast.

Mine is a really really beautiful music box, with a ballerina. I know why he's sent me this, it's because I love my Mammy's old music box, which plays a tune called Firedance. Martin thinks that if I have a musical box of my own, it will be a sort of almost-as-good thing. It isn't, but it's very nice and I'm very happy. Peter's present from Martin is a Swiss Army knife and he's really excited about it. Mum looks at us both and at Martin's brown paper around our feet and says 'Well, *we* needn't have bothered.'

I've written to Aunty Nelly, 'Please will you take this pony picture to Mammy's grave for me on Christmas day?' And Aunty Nelly wrote back that she'll take flowers and have a Mass said and light the candle in the shrine too. So Mammy will have a lovely Christmas in Heaven and know she's not forgotten. And then it bloody happens. It bloody happens.

At Christmas dinner, a friend from the Sergeant's Mess comes and his name is Norman. Norman and Dad have this funny pretend fight about saints and Dad sticks up for the church although he's usually at its throat, Mummy's smiling and shaking her head and Norman says something about Purgatory and Dad says 'Don't let's get started on that' but Norman goes off on one, for hours and hours about someone called Dante and fire and agony and how you suffer there for centuries and I say, and my voice has gone all small and hurting in my throat, 'For centuries?' And Norman says 'According to the Pope and his henchmen.' Daddy pours Norman another whisky and Mummy brings in some mince pies and Christmas falls away. Bloody stinking Christmas.

Centuries. My Mammy. There's me thinking it would just have been a few months.

Peter unpacks his case and packs it all up again and he keeps counting his money. Norman's given him two pounds and I gave him a shop bought card which says 'To a special brother'. Which he isn't. Mum's cut his hair and she says she's not got the back right but Dad says the Navy will cut it for him, and lower his ears, and that sounds awful but Norman laughs and so does Peter. He looks different now he's a sailor, and he's nicer, which is annoying because he'll soon be gone.

I watch Cheyenne when Mummy's sleeping and Dad's playing chess with Norman and Peter's packing up his old *Eagle* annuals for the church jumble, but there's a big rock where my heart used to be. Effing Purgatory. Centuries. My Mammy. Cheyenne reaches out from the TV and he says 'You alright?' And I say no, no I'm bloody not, I'm worried sick and wouldn't he be? and Cheyenne nods, because he's not a great one for words.

On Wednesday we all go to the station and wave Peter off because he starts his training straight after Christmas and Dad says it's a funny bloody day to start and they could have waited till New Year was over, but Peter's excited and you can tell he can't wait. He says if I cry he'll never forgive me so I don't very much and neither does he, very much.

On Thursday, New Year's Eve, Mummy and me go to Confession because Mummy says we all have to start the New Year in a state of grace. Daddy doesn't go to Confession or take Communion or anything but he does come to Mass so he's not in mortal sin, which is a relief, because I don't think I can pray for any more people. I don't know who the priest is, but he sounds fat and I can hear him breathing. I ask him how long we spend in Purgatory and he says it all depends on the sins we've committed and I say not many and he says 'A good Catholic?' And I say she was, yes, and the priest, behind his mesh, in the shadows and full of plumpness and knowing, says 'About forty years.'

Forty years. Forty buggering years. I kneel down to say my penance but instead I count them off on my fingers. Mammy's not been dead two years yet, thirty or something to go. Add eight which is how old I am. Nine. She'll get out of the furnace, all blistered and burnt, with her hair shrivelled up and frowsy and her eyelids gone, when I'm nearly forty or fifty or fifty-seven or something. Bloody God. I'm that mad.

I pull the leaves off the privet on the way home and kick stones, but Mummy doesn't say anything about ladies and ladylike, she's walking funny and holding her belly and biting her lip. When we get to the High Street Mummy stops and groans and does a wee right there in the road and that's the baby coming.

ANTHONY GERARD

I saw a picture once, I can't remember where, of a body on this metal table, just the bottom of the feet, the heels together and the toes at what Mummy calls 'a-quarter-to-three'. There was a luggage label around the big toe, but I haven't got any string so a man in a brown overall will have to do that in the morning, when they find me. I haven't even got a label. The brown overall makes me think of the big fat bastard in Omagh, and then the school caretaker. I'm glad it won't be him, with the sticky stuff in the corner of his mouth and the jokes no-one laughs at. Maybe Mr Mills from the undertakers will do it. Mr Mills who looked after baby Anthony and made him a little white coffin just the right size.

Mummy was in hospital three weeks and Anthony who was beautiful although I didn't see him till later, was in a special box so he could breathe, called an incubator. Daddy said he was a nice little lad. When Mummy came home, she had to leave him behind and I walked in from school one day and there she was, in her powder blue suit and very pale but smiley. She said we'd kept the house beautifully while she was away and I asked if I could visit Anthony now because I used to visit my Mammy so I'm good at being quiet and nice to the nurses but Daddy said no, Anthony's too ill and there's only an hour visiting a day and they need it. So I said OK.

When he was four weeks old they took out his lung, one of them and it's the first time anyone's done that to such a tiny baby

51

and the operation was a success but everyone was still very sad, so I sort of knew. When he was six weeks old, Anthony died.

He came home for one night and Daddy carried his coffin up to Peter's room, which was going to be his if he'd lived. Then they said I could go up. I took my best drawing for the baby, because there was nothing else I could take to show him I loved him. The tiny coffin was in the middle of the room and there were bunches of flowers, white roses, white freesias for the little dead baby, dressed all in white, with a small flower on his Peter Pan collar. I can remember Mummy sewing it. He was beautiful.

We stood there, in sad adoration. Like the three kings. And you could hear us all breathing and that made it sort of harder that the wee baby was stone still. I put a hand out and touched the coffin. I love you. I love you. If I could grab you up and run off with you.... if I could give you my breath..... take you home and love you back to life. If I could vanish and you could be here instead of me. You and your Mummy, loving you. Holding you. Your perfect Mummy, with her perfect baby, and my Daddy smiling, happy.

I said, 'He's the most beautiful beautiful baby in the whole wide world.' and I didn't even know I was doing it. My hand stretched out. I touched Anthony's hair. There was this noise, and it was Mummy, and Dad grabbed her because her legs went bendy and I said 'Sorry.' And she said 'Get away from him. Don't touch him.' And Dad had an arm around her and his other arm around me, pulling me away, but I was stepping back anyway and I kept saying 'Sorry' and he said 'It's alright' but Mummy just kept on 'I don't want her near him, get her away.'

I tried to go out but before I could, she grabbed my pony drawing and shoved it in my face and then in Dad's and he was sort of leaning back but still holding her and she was crying, proper snotty crying. 'Look what I've got. Look - a dead baby, and that great lump and her bloody drawing of another bloody pony. Look at what I've bloody got.'

Perfect little face. Little white hands. Little wax nails. A perfect Mummy and Daddy. A shiny little family. It should be me in a coffin and he should be in his little cot with the blanket she knitted. Dear God, please let it be me. Take me now... You can do it. Please. Please. Give me back to my Mammy and give him back to his. Please.

But nothing happened. So here I am. You can die of the cold. Like that man in the North Pole with ice in his beard.

I've put the blankets right down at the bottom of the bed and I've opened the window and now, with my heels touching and my feet flopping like a seal's flippers, I begin to die, which isn't easy at the best of times, and sometimes it's so difficult that I'm halfway to school before I remember that I didn't even reach my knees the night before. Dying of the cold is a good way of dying because if you drown it's terrible frightening and you fight and shout and try to live, but if you die of the cold you just go to sleep. Someone said. We go to sleep every night so this sort of dying would be no big thing. Sometimes I manage to stay awake until the cold has reached my middle. I know that if ever I could think the cold right up past my kidneys, as they float in a small sea of golden wee somewhere near my belly, and up past my heart, and all the tubes that run up inside my neck, to my porridge brain, I'd have done it at last. In the morning there would be only an alabaster face on a white pillow and blue fingernails and a space where I used to be, right up to the empty sky. And then they'll be sorry.

Tonight dying of the cold is harder than usual because Maigret's on the telly downstairs and he looks a bit like Dad, and a bit like Harry Secombe and they're my favourite people. When I close my eyes I can't shut out the rumble of voices, Dad's and the policeman's, who is only an actor, and Mummy's, all mixed up. I blocked my ears once but in the morning Mummy found the chewed up ear-hole plugs on the pillow and Dad discovered the missing blank page at the back of *Alice Through the Looking Glass*, torn out in wanton vandalism. If I hum 'Danny Boy', I won't hear Dad stirring his tea eight times and chink-chink-chink-ing the spoon on the rim of the cup which should be cheerful but it reminds me how far away he is, a floor, a ceiling, a staircase far below. Sometimes dying of cold starts to work straight away, and I can't feel my toes, or the bed or anything at all, but some nights nothing much happens and even asking the Blessed Virgin or Saint Sebastian, the patron saint of the dying, doesn't help. I go up a mountain in my head, or to the North Pole where people die all the time, with dogs and balaclavas, and they eat Mars Bars instead of proper meals. And the Mars Bars ruin everything because they make me wonder how many I could buy if I had a whole pound and I have to start again. Only cold. Only think of cold. And don't move. Don't think. People die of the cold, and that's a fact.

The baby was cold. I knew he wasn't going to be warm but I didn't know he'd be ice cold. Cold and white and doll perfect, half Norah and half Dad, a little heart-shaped mouth and a long neck where I don't have any. 'No neck, no waist or hips or anything, not a bone in her,' Mummy said when we had to find something to wear at the funeral. Dad said 'Puppy fat' and Mummy looked at my feet and said that thing about quarter to three and I knew that every bit of me was wrong and there was nothing I could do about it. She doesn't look at me, just my feet and my bum and my knees.

Martin and Peter came home on passionate leave just for the funeral day, and they looked so handsome in their uniforms and I kept thinking 'Mammy and Anthony would be very proud' and that seemed sad, like they'd put on their uniforms and pressed their trousers and Peter's bell bottoms, which are magnificent, for a Mammy and a baby who would never see them. It would be good if you could send a photo to Heaven but you can't, so it's no good dwelling on it, which Daddy says sometimes. You just have to get on with it.

Think cold. Hum your hum and close your eyes and think cold. Lie down and die, you bugger, which is what Uncle Alf said to Mr Harrison when he fell down in our jitty, drunk again. Shut up about Uncle Alf. Cold.

The night has gone when I wake up, and the TV is off. I stay there for a whole minute, counting seconds, listening, but the ceiling is above me, not the sky, not the satin cushion of a coffin lid, not a doctor shaking his head. And I can blink. And then I can move my hand and my head. Not dead, then, and Dad shaving in the bathroom and my school clothes waiting at the end of the bed. When I pull on my socks I let out a bugger. And then a bloody. Buggering bloody hell. Not dead again.

On the way to school, Danny Boy is here, walking in step, going on and on with his singing, which is a pain because I'm praying to Saint Theresa, who's going to be one of my confirmation names, promising to eat all my cauliflower cheese, which is slimy and makes me whump, if we can just have 'Faith Of Our Fathers' with its dungeons, fires and swords for assembly.

Oh Danny boy, the pipes, the pipes are calling
From glen to glen, and down the mountain side
The summer's gone, and all the flowers are dying
'Tis you, 'tis you must go and I must bide.

Bum. Go away, Danny. You're all muddled up with Bobby Shafto anyway, and Bonnie Prince Charlie. I'm not sure why. It might be something to do with the buckles on his knee. Like that painting of the Blue Boy, only he's got ribbons, not buckles. And he looks like a girl. I've forgotten what I was thinking now.

And this is lovely. This is lovely life and laughing and singing songs too loud and shouting and forgetting everything. This is school and school is lovely. Running across the playground, followed by an army, all shouting and screaming and the boys chasing the girls and the girls screaming and screaming and climbing up the milk crates by the kitchen where a dinner lady is putting on her pinny and she bangs on the window and mouths 'No!' and everyone laughs when Davey Williams shouts 'Poo knickers!' but she can't hear so he blows her a kiss and she shakes her head, smiling, and turns away. The army swoops down past the bins and up across the grass bank and down again into the infants' playground, like a great swarm of swallows, or bees, or a whole Heaven full of happy whooping angels. This is school and it's lovely. I could live here for ever and never ever go to sleep, I could eat mashed potato and cabbage and listen to Mrs Atherton reading and sniff up the smells of the cloakroom, right up into my nose, for ever and never want to be dead again. I could.

He looks a bit like Tommy Steele, does Danny Boy. He's been waiting by the gates all day and sometimes, when I was queuing up to have my spelling marked or to get a pencil sharpened, I looked out, on tip toe, and there he was, lighting a fag, turning into Elvis Presley and then back into Tommy Steel because Danny Boy, who was Irish, could have ginger hair and freckles, which Dad says is Protestant, or black hair and blue eyes, which is Catholic, or he could be fair, like Bobby Shafto who was Scottish or something, and Scottish is nearly Irish anyway.

No one else has Danny Boy to walk home with. I asked Susan Matkin if she could make up people and she said no one can. So it's only me and that's one in the eye for the whole bloody lot of them.

And if you come, when all the flowers are dying
And I am dead, as dead I well may be
You'll come and find the place where I am lying
And kneel and say an 'Ave' there for me.

We dawdle home as slow as we can go, because home is sad now and a sort of nothing place to be, and I wonder where, in the song, Danny Boy was supposed to be going, while whoever it was stayed at home and died. There won't be anyone who will kneel where I lie and say anything at all for me. Dad could, but I know he won't. When Mammy died he didn't kneel and say an Ave where she lay. He said 'Come on, then, let's do some sorting out, shall we?' He didn't pray or cry or anything for the baby either, Anthony Gerard, born December 30th, died February 14th. Valentine's day. When they got to the bit in the funeral about 'life's little day', Mummy let out this mangled sort of cry and Dad grabbed her and I can still hear that sound now and see his white knuckles on her elbow as he helped her to sit down, in the pew, beside the little white coffin. And when they took it out to the grave, with Dad carrying it, I didn't know where to stand and Martin and Peter were standing at sort of attention but I felt stupid because I didn't have a uniform and I'm only a little girl so I got in the way and Mummy looked at me and then looked away as if she couldn't bear it, and she couldn't, and neither could I. Couldn't bear that the new-made baby was going into the dirt and this great ugly thing was filling up the space where he should be living and growing and being the apple of his Daddy's eye. Which is what it says on the gravestone they've ordered. He was the apple of my eye too.

After the funeral there wasn't any sandwiches or anything because Mummy didn't want people and she went into the presbytery with Daddy and the priest. Martin and Peter and me walked home and Peter told us all about HMS Ganges and Martin told us all about Belfast and I walked between them and remembered walking between Mummy and Daddy in Golborne that time, and I wondered how everything had gone so wrong so quickly.

Peter had to go straight back to Portsmouth and when we got to the house he said he wouldn't even come in for a cup of tea and that he didn't even want to come at all, but Daddy wrote to his petty officer, which is what they are sometimes in the Navy, and they said he had to come or else. So we walked to the station with him but he said for crying out loud don't come onto the platform because this fucking family's had enough tearful farewells so we didn't. I wish he'd stop being so angry with me because I haven't done anything.

They call them petty officers because they are very small, like Nelson, who had a jacket which would fit a ten year old boy. Mr Bentley told us in assembly on Nelson's birthday or death day or something. He wanted to tell us that even small people can be big heroes.

Martin and me walked home and Martin put the kettle on and I started to get a bit worried but then Mummy and Daddy came in and Mummy went to bed. We had fish and chips, just the three of us and it was almost happy. It was happy. It was lovely sitting with Daddy and Martin and listening, but we all knew Mummy was upstairs crying so every time we laughed we sort of muffled it and stopped it short and took a breath.

I counted the cards Mummy got and there are twenty-nine, and there's one from Aunty Nelly and Uncle Alf. Condolences, and two boney hands joined together like they're praying.

That was weeks ago. Life's little day. I keep thinking that and I don't know why. Sometimes you get words stuck in your head.

THE THREE OF US

After Anthony died Daddy drew all the curtains and said we had to be quiet for a while so we were. We didn't have the radio on or anything. And after the funeral when Martin had gone back to Belfast, Daddy opened the curtains and said I could watch *Children's Hour* if I had the sound down low. I must stay out of Mummy's way and make myself as quiet as a mouse and then everything will gradually get better, he said.

I heard Daddy on the phone, and he was talking to Norman, because that's how they play chess now they don't see each other every week, with Anthony and everything. But when he wasn't saying all the pawn to rook Bishop three things, he was saying 'Good of you to ring.' And then there was this long time when Norman was speaking and Dad made a little yes sound which wasn't yes but was just to let Norman know he was still there, listening.

I turned the sound right down on the telly and crept to the door to listen. Daddy said 'No, no chance. They had to take it all away. Yes.' Norman must have said something because Dad sighed and then said 'Yes, that's it. For Norah and me. There's just going to be the two of us.' and Norman said something else and then Dad said 'Of course. And her.' I turned the telly up again and it was *The Lone Ranger* but I didn't see it or hear it, I just sat in front of it, and got a headache.

I walk myself to school now and I walk myself home, which

sounds like I push myself in a wheelbarrow, but that would be impossible. It just means I don't go with anyone. Everything has changed. Daddy says I have to be as quiet as a church mouse. Church mice are poor, but I know what he meant and I didn't say anything. When I let myself into the house I can hear Mum in the kitchen. I don't go through because Mum can only think of one thing at a time and there's no room anyway. My job is to stay out of the way, make myself as small as possible, and be seen and not heard. Or not even be seen. Something like that. Uncle Alf used to say – it doesn't matter what he used to say. I don't think about that any more.

There's a new list propped up by the stairs. It's called a to-do list. Every Monday there's a new one. At first I can't see what's different from the old one, so I stand there, with my quarter-to-three feet pooling invisible me-stain on the carpet that has to last at least ten years, worrying that Mum will want to know what I'm up to and then all the thoughts will fall out of my head and my tongue will stick to the roof of my mouth and Mum will save it up for when Dad comes home and say 'Why is she always so sullen, Gerry?' and Dad will say 'I don't know.' in his I-give-up voice. It's because sometimes I can't talk. Everyone else can talk, every day, but there are some days when I can't talk at all. Not even a word. The doctor said, in Golborne, the one who had a box of Quality Street on his desk, that it was a phrase.

There were nine little lines of words on the list yesterday and today it's gone up to eleven. Number one, outdoor clothes off and hung up. Number two, outdoor shoes off and slippers on. And then there's a new one; 'Notes from school to be placed on the hall table' and then another new one 'do NOT turn the radio on'. I look at it, the tiny words, the angry capital letters of NOT, the empty little circle, full stops at the end of each line, the neat ring around each number. I wish I couldn't read. Then she'd have to tell me.

Open the kitchen door and tell me. But I only half want her to. The other half of me wants to kill her. I wish I was in Golborne, even with Uncle Alf. That was only sometimes. This is always. And Aunty Nelly was there with her Mr Chop, the butcher's legs and her lap to sit on and her shoulder to rest on and here there's just me and lilac fucking walls. The F word. A small lump of sadness rises in my throat, like a smooth grey pebble that chokes me and hurts when I try to swallow it. I've stopped calling Mummy Mummy and I'm glad. It's not so much like Mammy, if you say Mum. And it doesn't hurt so much when Mum looks at me. And I'm nearly ten anyway, so it's more grown up.

Danny's stayed outside. Or gone back up to Heaven or something. I'm not daft, I know they're not real but I make them real so they are in a way. My way. Anyway, none of them like being in the house much, not Danny Boy or Cheyenne Bodie, or Heidi. Well, I know Heidi's a made-up person, so she isn't in Heaven, and I know too that Cheyenne is an actor, a man called Clint who lives in California round the corner from Perry Mason who is a man called Raymond. But Danny Boy was real once so when he's not here he's up in Heaven, like Mammy, and he might be up there now, watching me, but I hope not because number seven on the list is 'open your bowels' and I don't want my guardian angel and all the other angels and Mammy and the panoply of saints watching that. And God.

Your bowels are like bellows, which is why the word is the same but different, and sometimes it doesn't matter how hard I fill my bellows with great grunts of air, pushing and pushing until I go red, and my head pounds and bursts, nothing will happen. And then I have to go downstairs and say 'No go. Sorry.' although I'm not sorry at all, but Mum sighs and slams a saucepan and then a cupboard door, and says she does her best but it's an uphill task and God help me when

I get older. Bellows and bowels have the same letters as elbows, but that might not mean much. Dad says it's all to do with Mum once being an important nurse, in charge of bedpans. I thought he was joking but when I laughed Mum looked away and it turns out she was really important and saved lives on a daily basis.

At tea, I ask Dad what an uphill task is, and he says 'Sisyphus. Look it up at school.' and I'm going to say that the school doesn't let us look things up, but as I take a breath to make the words Mum says if I've finished I can leave the table and let them have some peace. There's rice pudding cooling on the side, the skin golden, but I thank Mum for a lovely tea, which it wasn't, and push my chair back to the table, and I know that everything I do makes her wicked stepmotherly heart bang and her teeth grind. The chair knocks the table, Mum goes stiff and I get this tiny mean voice in my head saying 'serves-you-right'. I go to take my plate with its knife and fork through to the kitchen, like always, but the knife slips and the fork clatters and Dad puts a hand out and stops them landing on the table. 'For God's sake' Mum says, without opening her lips or making any sound at all. I look at her, and Dad says 'Leave them. Just bloody leave them.' So I do.

I stand outside the dining room door again, picking the wallpaper, listening to their conversation, lumpy with short laughs, sighs and murmurs, waiting for them to say something about me, so that I'll know that when I'm not there, I'm still here. Sometimes, with the numbers galloping in my brain and the uphill struggle and the feet and everything, it feels like, when I'm not there, I'm not anywhere. As if I'm like Heidi, an idea on a page, a memory from someone's head, maybe a thought Mammy once had, and now Mammy's no more than a thought I once had. Someone moves in the room and I quickly step away and onto the stairs and stay there, heart thumping, but no one comes and I quietly, carefully, creep upwards, like Tonto. Without even treading on a twig.

I take out my writing pad to start a letter to Martin. I don't write to Peter because he never writes to me and Daddy makes a joke of it and says nearly every day 'Another deluge of correspondence from Peter, I see.' Which is the unfunniest joke the world has ever known because we haven't heard from him since the funeral and he could be dead too for all we know. Two dead brothers. It's beyond a joke.

Dear Martin

Thank you for your letter. I don't have any news except Father Sullivan said to tell you that Wigan and St Helen's was a terrible game and Wigan lost and were a shambles. Did you bet him five bob that Wigan would be champions because he said it's as good as in his back pocket already. Lots of love Lucy

Dear Aunty Nelly,

Thank you for the Bunty, it is smashing and I've read it three times. The four Marys are my favourite because my Mammy was Mary and my middle name is Mary. Last week Daddy was away on an exercise on Salisbury Plain so Norah and me had scrambled eggs. She says she is better and thank you for the card.

We are all well. Please scratch Kitty Lob's ear for me. Lots of love Lucy

When I write to Aunty Nelly I call Mum Norah because I feel bad about her missing her sister who was my Mammy and I don't want her to think that I've forgotten Mammy, because although I can't remember her, I'll never forget her. If I wrote to Peter, which I don't, I'd call her Norah in those letters too, because when he heard me calling her Mummy he went lunatic. And that was when he got that stutter and Dad said bloody hell what was wrong with all his children, were we emotional cripples? Some days I can't quite manage words. Talking. And then he joined the Navy. Not Dad, Peter. Sometimes I have to remember these things in my head because so much has happened I keep forgetting.

Even though the curtains are open and I can watch an hour of telly every day, the house is a creeping quiet place.

I had what I thought was a very good thought yesterday or today or sometime, and that is that if Mammy was in the next room, I wouldn't be sad or missing her, I'd just be thinking 'Mammy's in the next room, so what?' But then that made me want her too much and cry so I had to stop. If you do your thinking properly, it's OK. You just have to stop the thinking that hurts and gives you a sore throat. I wonder if everyone is like me or if I'm not like anyone. I think I'm not like anyone.

Mum's Dad, who is not my Grandfather but I have to call him that, and Mum's Mum who I call Grandma, came to stay from Brighton where they live. They are very old, older than Aunty Nelly. Grandad said he wanted to give me something and asked me what I wanted and I said a crossbow, like William Tell and he looked at Mum and said 'Isn't that a strange thing for a little girl to want?' And Mum said 'She's a strange little girl.' And they both looked at me like they were thinking. So that's how I know I'm not like anyone. I'd seen a crossbow in a shop in Warminster and we went there, me and Daddy and it was five shillings. It's green and metal and I shoot the trees in the garden for hours and hours, with William Tell, and Daddy says at least it keeps me out from under. If I go out after lunch I can come back in at four o clock, if I go straight to my room and don't get in anyone's way.

FMUMMMF

It's a field, just a bloody old field, and there's a horse and it's got its head down, nibbling the grass. I can hear the crunch, the roots of the grass breaking, the clunk clunk of the big yellow teeth. It's a nice horse. And the sun's shining and it all starts off happy but with this feeling, a sort of knowing without knowing, like the night Mammy died. And the knowing grows bigger, like an Army truck on Salisbury Plain, so it's tiny and silent and a dot on the grey ribbon road and you don't hardly see it but it gets bigger and noisier until it batters you with a great rush of wind like in *The Wizard of Oz*, which I saw and loved but Dad calls it yankee rubbish. And suddenly it's there, the knowing, and I know it. That bloody horse is on my Mammy's grave. There's no stone, no dearly loved wife, beloved mother, no flowers, no little green stones, no nothing, but I know. She's there in her pale ivory silk and satin coffin, feets below. And I try to run to the horse and pull it away but my feet are stuck and my mouth won't open to let the shouting out so I stand there, waving my arms through air like treacle, and a fmummmf soft strangled sound in my throat and the horse just chews. And chews. And no one's bloody there to help.

I'm that sick of that dream. That and the Uncle Alf dream. If I could stay awake for ever.

There's a graveyard in the town and they've moved all the stones to round the edge so you don't know where the graves are any more, and Alison Carter said they're going to dig up the bodies because they want a bowling green instead. And Ginger Neil said they won't, they've done it so they can start all over again, putting new bodies in on top of the old ones and sticking up new stones. Ginger Neil said Frankenstein was made from old bodies but I said Frankenstein is the doctor because I've read the book and he gave me a Chinese burn so I gave him one back. Mammy's buried in Newton Le Willows which is miles and miles away from where we are now so how will I ever know if they do something to her grave? Alison said they dig people up after fifty years and in China they bury people standing up to save room and I slapped her, and she called me a cow. I think that's when the dreams started. They stay with me all day sometimes and the world feels full of sadness, badness, madness.

You know when that shark bites with his teeth,
Babe,
Scarlet billows start to spread

That's a song Dad sings and then he pretends to put gloves on and he goes all scarey and Mum laughs and is pretty again and it's almost like the baby isn't dead, for just a minute. But he is. We all laugh when he sings it but it's not a happy laugh from me, it's a strange laugh and I feel a bit scared.

I don't tell anyone about the horse. It's hard enough being a step mother without me forever moaning on and I don't know how lucky I am. So I don't say anything. When it wakes me up, the horse, or Uncle Alf, or anything, I say a decade of the Rosary for Mammy's soul. She's been in Purgatory nearly three years and little Anthony's been in Limbo six months. He doesn't need a prayer because Limbo's like a nursery, like Andy Pandy's garden, with talking flowers and Looby Lou, but I say one anyway. The big news is that I've got to take the Eleven Plus and if I pass I'll wear a straw hat called a boater and go to a convent in Bath where the nuns are French but they're all healthy bog girls from Ireland. Which is so much nonsense, like *Alice in Wonderland* which I've got round to reading because Dad kept asking me questions about it. It's rubbish.

I sit on my bed and look at my alarm clock. Half past six. Bed in an hour. To give them some life of their own, and I'm not even tired, I haven't even yawned. I could make William Tell appear, who – the actor – is a friend of a friend Mum once knew, called Conrad someone and I've told everyone at school but no one believes me. Jennifer Ainsley said 'And is he related to Uncle Winston Churchill too?' which I ignored like Sophia Stanton Lacey in *The Grand Sophy*.

I wonder, again, if I could be a made up person in someone's book, but I don't think so, because most of the time nothing happens, and in books something happens all the time, every day, or there would be books full of pages and pages of nothing and there aren't any books like that. Apart from exercise books. Which are different. And if I was a made up person in a book there wouldn't be so much of me, always getting in the way and blocking the light. I would be written thinner, maybe with an empress line dress and ringlets and a fan and young officers wanting to dance with me. Or Beth in *Little Women*, sweet and pale and tragic. The good thing about being me is that no one will miss me and there will be no hole where I used to be, just a piece of grey air to fill up my foot prints. Mrs Gordon, our teacher, will be a bit sad, but if no one's off sick they're a desk short, so she'll soon see the good side of it and will say that it's a blessing really, like Mammy was, but I never thought that, no matter how many people said it.

It was Aunty Nelly who told me about the dead souls going up into Heaven and the unborn souls coming to find new born babies, when we walked home from evening Mass and the sun was going down behind clouds and there were all these shafts of light and she said 'That's the way souls come and go' and it makes perfect sense when you think of it. Which I do quite often. And if it works, me going up to Heaven so the baby can come down on one of those shafts of light, Mum will have him to love, a perfect little baby with five-to-twelve feet, and he'll be Dad's consolation too, which is what Canon Castledine said he needs now, some consolation, because he's had some hard knocks. The great thing of it, the Canon said, is that, being a child, I will bounce back none the worse. I don't think I've bounced back yet.

I'm not absolutely sure it will work, me going up and Anthony coming down, but when I asked Mrs Atherton if prayers always get answered she said they do if we have faith enough, even if we think they haven't been. And something about eight Romans being good to the Lord or something. And I have faith, and I'm trying to get even more, day by day, by practising believing. I can believe almost anything now, if I really try, and when I said this to Father Sullivan he bit his lip and swallowed and said I'd go far and called me Alice, who I happen to know is a girl with long hair so it's a clever thing to say but it's not that clever. Or if it is, it must have been a bit I skipped. I hate those books.

I don't hear Dad coming up the stairs and when he knocks on the door and pokes his head in, I jump. He never comes to my room any more and he isn't here now really, his mind already back downstairs with Mum. He doesn't notice that I'm sitting on the bed without a book or anything, he just stands there, in the doorway, looking sad. Norah finds me difficult. I'm not sure what to say so I don't say anything. He sighs. I have to be a good girl and try to make things easier for everyone. Norah's such a good person and she's hurting still, quite badly. He changes that to 'very deeply' and we must all try to understand. Mustn't we? I nod. He looks relieved and for a moment I think he's going to kiss me but he just winks and says 'Good girl' and goes.

And suddenly I see myself, sitting there, all alone in a room with lilac walls, which I full-blooded hate, and everything tidy. Just me in nothing. And it's as sad as the 'Soldier's Farewell', which is a picture in *King Arthur's Treasury*. I look at it when I want to have a little weep and feel better after. But I don't want to have a little weep now so I look at the happy picture of Mammy holding me when I'd just been born and I'm frowning up into Mam's face, squinty and new, and Mammy's smiling at the camera, and I can see the little fat ears that no one else has and if I stare at it till it goes all blurred, my eyes meet her eyes and Mammy doesn't start and I don't end and we're just the one and I can feel her, the smell and the nearness of her. I swallow hard and my eyes prick, but I mustn't start because once I start I won't be able to stop until I'm hiccupping and sick and swallowing my snot and sobbing and hiccupping again and coughing and can't breathe.

Maybe I should pray that I won't have been born at all. That God will take time back and someone else will be born instead of me. But then this prayer wouldn't be a real prayer. I wouldn't exist to ask God to unborn me. So that won't work. If I'm going to Heaven I'll have to take myself there. I take a big breath and a last look at Mammy's picture.

No one calls out to me as I walk down the stairs. The front door opens and closes silently, and Danny Boy glides out of the shadows to join me as we walk away. The streets smell different at night. It's almost dark, and lights are going on in the houses we pass. I look in and see an old man poking a fire, and in the next house a woman painting a wall. A television is warming up in the third, watched by two children. I know them, both serious little speccy-four-eyes with bottle green knitted jumpers and grey socks. His name is Eric and he has wet lips and little white shiny spots on his nose. Her name is Winnie and she has long plaits and reads a book a day and her Gran says she's a pinch off being a genius. I stand watching until the picture stops rolling and Cliff Michelmore is looking at me, over the path and across the garden, and through the window. The next tonight will be tomorrow night. I'm allowed to watch him on Fridays, when there's no school the next day, and I can stay up until eight o clock. I like the long thin man with the Scottish accent who walks along the road looking murderous but then he smiles and it's alright. Mum has a crush on Michelmore, that's what Dad always says, but Mum laughs her best laugh and hits him and they end up pushing and shoving and laughing some more and I have to look away before Mum sees me watching and I ruin it all for everyone, again.

In Park Road, Cheyenne Bodie joins us and Mrs Walters is on the step, shouting Theresa in for tea. It makes me think of Aunty Nelly banging a saucepan with her wooden spoon and yelling 'Grub's up' and I laugh. Then I remember that I'm still wearing my slippers, and my cardigan with no coat, and I wonder what I'll say if anyone stops me. But Theresa, who is wild and angry and a little bit not right in the head, charges past and up the steps and shouts a wordless word as the door slams behind her and the street settles down to dusty silence again. In a few steps me and Danny Boy have turned off Station Road, and on up the road past the school, blind-eyed now and twice as big. No one can see us because we are invisible. Maybe I've been a bit invisible ever since Mammy gave up the ghost.

I start to sing, but my voice is wavery bat squeaks in the echoey

streets, so I swop from 'Living Doll' to 'Jerusalem', which is
Protestant but brave and fierce, but my voice keeps tailing off into
nothing so I stop. I'm taking a breath for 'Faith Of Our Fathers'
which needs a damn good lungful says Mr Bentley, but we're
passing a baker's and Mammy used to work in a baker's for a bit
of extra Christmas money, and I have to look away or I'll see the
memory of her in the big wide window and if I start to cry now it
will take me over entirely and turn me inside out, and put all the
snot and the spit and coughing on the outside where it shouldn't
be and my poor heart will choke on it all, which is the worst a soul
can suffer. Worse than the nuns in the Congo who had their breasts
chopped off, worse than Catherine who was tied to a firework,
worse than Stephen or any of them. Maybe not worse than the
nuns, but bad enough for a child of eight. Nine. Ten, for God's
sake. I was eight for such a long time I keep forgetting.

When we get to the shoe factory, I stop a minute, trying to
make up my mind. The church is a long walk away through the
old streets, or twice as far if you follow the main road which is all
lit by big yellow street lights and not at all scarey. It's not so far
down the jittys. I take a deep breath and hug my chest and put my
head down and run. Danny Boy has gone but Cheyenne is still
there, pounding along beside me, loping, a hand on his six gun,
eyes scanning the rooftops for wolves. And Indians, wild with war
paint. When I get a stitch he waits, sort of dancing on his toes, like
a boxer, patiently, hands hovering over his holster, silent and ever
watchful. By the time we reach the church it's the dead of night,
and I'm surprised to see lights on. The big heavy doors stand open
and the smaller glass ones inside the porch are unlocked so I
quietly turn the handle and go in. The church is yellow bright with
all the lights blazing, and a few people are in the pews, mostly
kneeling, heads bowed, a scattering of headscarves and old men's

necks. Confession. I'd forgotten about that. I dip my fingertips in the holy water and do 'spectacles, testicles, wallet and watch', bold and wicked. An old woman smiles at me as she goes out, a sweet old smile, and I wish I'd done the sign of the cross properly but it's too late now.

The woman from the sweet shop is lighting a candle for Our Lady, probably for her son who isn't the full shilling and shouts at cars, hopeless yearning shouts of 'I can drive, I can!' and 'Change up! Change up!' like he knows what he's on about. She slipped me a Penny Arrow toffee bar once, for free, and maybe that's one of the reasons she's lighting that candle. Atonement for her sin. I get a sudden horrible stomach plunging thought – I took the toffee and ate it, and now I'm not totally completely sure if I ever confessed it. Bugger. I thought I was sin free, bound for Heaven with maybe a little bit in Purgatory on the way, nowhere near forty years, but now I've got the toffee to worry about, and a bugger, and this morning's bloody buggering too. Shit. Stop it. Like the boy shouting at cars, I can't stop. Fuck. Now I'm up shit creek for sure. Bugger. Give over. I rub my forehead, and pinch my cheek hard, to stop the words. Bum bum bum, which shouldn't really be a swear word because it's just a bit of the body and we all have one, even the Queen. Even Jesus. That's bloody done it. Give over. The more I bloody try the harder it fucking is.

Dear God, bloody hell.

As soon as I go into the confessional I know it's Father Sullivan. I can smell the Polo mints. I count the number of times he says 'My dearly beloved brethren' when he gives a sermon and the record is seventeen. He closes his eyes too, when he's in the pulpit, so he won't have to see everyone, staring at him, in the pews, and you can see him sweating as he rocks on his toes. Dad says he should never have gone into the church but he was the youngest son and the Irish are savages. The youngest son and the ugly girls, he said, they get sent to the church whether they want to or not. Dad is Irish, which makes me Irish, so I think we're probably savages too. 'Bless me Father, for I have sinned, it is four days since my last confession.' The priest breathes out, like he's happy and I can see his shadow on the mesh, leaning forward, a smile in his voice, 'Welcome, my child.' That's the best bit of the confession, that is. None of the other priests say it. Father Donoghue takes no interest in your sins at all and then he batters you with the biggest penance ever – crawl to Rome on your bare knees or something, and Canon Castledine groans when you can't remember how many times you wished Veronica next door was dead.

I have sworn, several times, in my head, and three times out loud, and slammed a door, and lied about my bowels. Father Sullivan says 'Anything else, my child?' and I tell him about the Penny Arrow and that it might be already forgiven and he says you can forgive something twice, not to worry. I don't mean to, but I tell him that I ruin everything for everyone and I have the manners of a bear and the sight of me makes Mum sick but I can't do anything about that and if I could I bloody would. And there's a little sharp silence, and I say sorry about the B word, and there's a funny noise from the other side of the mesh, and Father Sullivan says 'You're alright, Lucy Gannon.' And I wonder how he knew it was me.

Three Hail Mary's isn't bad. I kneel down and sing-song through them, my head bowed but peeping out through my fingers, watching the feet of the other sinners as one by one they genuflect and leave. When the last one has gone into the confessional, and everyone else has left, I quickly slip into Saint Joseph's little corner, which no one ever goes to, him being just someone's husband and not the real thing at all. He's long and thin, is Joseph, and no good for hiding behind so I step out again and dodge behind Saint Francis of Assisi who has a deer and lambs around him, and a sparrow with no head on his outstretched hand, and I crouch down. I put a finger to my lips, 'Not a sound, Kemo Sabby' and the Lone Ranger nods and steps back into the shadows behind The Infant of Padua.

After absolutely ages the last one comes out of the confessional and though he must have had a hundred sins to tell, he just walks out of the church without stopping for a Hail Mary or a How's Your Father or anything. His footsteps ring out in the high space, like a soldier marching, the rhythm breaking when he stops to dip in the holy water. After another couple of minutes, Father Sullivan comes out and glances around. I try not to hold my breath because if you do that you make a noise when you start again. He genuflects and bows his head, a long prayer sort of genuflection. He goes to the back of the church, where I can't see him, and I hear the clanking and rattling and slamming of the outer doors being shut and barred, and then the rattle of the inside doors, the sound of the key turning, and then he walks back towards the altar but he turns suddenly, and stops in front of Saint Francis. I can't help holding my breath now, rigid, just an arm's length away from the Father's legs in their shiny black priest's trousers. Without moving a muscle, I roll my eyes and check that no bit of me is sticking out. How long do priests pray for? What if he does a whole decade of the Rosary? How can I hold my breath for all that time? What if I get cramp? What if – but Father Sullivan closes his eyes, and sighs, and says, aloud and all hollow and fed up 'That's it. You get on and feed the fucking animals. Never mind poor bloody suffering humanity.' I forget to hold my breath and I hear my own gasp, but I'm so busy thinking about Father Sullivan saying the F word that I don't even care, and anyway, he's gone, striding up the aisle towards the altar. He genuflects again and this time stays down even longer, a long long moment. And now he's walking through the vestry and the church is plunged into thick treacle darkness, and I'm blind. I listen as another door opens and closes in the distance and I know he's in the presbytery, and I hope he has a good supper waiting for him and a telly and a roaring fire.

I stay very still, Cheyenne Bodie, half Injun, half white man, half American. Listening, making sure. There's no sound. But then I see a shadow, a golden moving lightness across the blanket black. I poke my head out from behind the deer, very slowly. A way off, in the Lady Chapel, two candles are still alight, flickering and rising and falling and casting a small circle of light around Mary's plaster feet in golden slippers. I wish I'd thought to bring my seven and thruppence from my jewels box. I could have lit a lot of candles for my Mammy with that and it would have been my very last chance, what with me heading off to join her in Purgatory this very night. That's what they say in books. 'This very night'. I've never said it before but now it's just right for the very night I am in.

In her arms. Think of that. With her, with her, with her. A chorus of delight. And if the flames are licking right up us, blistering and sheer agony like Canon Castledine says, we won't care. Mammy will just hold me tight and whisper 'Soon be done,' and 'There's my girl' and thinking about it hurts so much and it's so lovely. I bite my lip, hard, as hard as I can.

I walk slowly, silent in my slippers, to the Communion rail, and to the centre, where the aisles meet in a crossroads. I kneel down first but it's hard on your knees and you'd topple over when you died so I lie on my front. Hands down by my side. I turn my head to the side, so that my cheek is on the cold stone. This is where the coffin was all night. This is where Mammy lay the night before the funeral. There must be tiny bits of her on the stone, little flakelets of skin or used up breath, that trickled through the wood and onto the ground beneath. I'd like to lick the stone but there will be other people's flakes too, other people's dead breath, there's little Anthony's for a start, because for every birth there has to be a death or the world would be teeming like the football games or those pictures of the trains in India. Stop thinking now. Stop.

And anyway, Mammy wasn't here, was she, you eedjit, she was there, with Aunty Nelly, and Uncle Alf and *Sunday Night at the London Palladium*, up there in Golborne. So there isn't even a breath of her left to share. Not here. So I'm glad I didn't lick the floor.

And if you come, when all the flowers are dying And I am dead, as dead I well may be

I'm getting a headache now. Or a toothache. Something.

If you'll not fail to tell me that you love me I'll simply sleep in peace until you come to me.

Being dead is like the dentists when he gives you gas. And it smells lovely, and then it smells horrible and like rubber, and then everything goes mumbled and grey and then you don't care and it's lovely again and you don't mind about the rubber smell. When they took my abscess out I thought I was gliding down this long staircase on a tea tray. I don't think being dead is like that.

And I am dead, as dead I well may be

And then you're on the bus on the way home and your mouth tastes like iron and you're being sick. No, not that bit. Being dead isn't that bit, on the bus. It's the first bit, the mumbled lovely bit. I think.

If you'll not fail to tell me that you love me, I'll simply sleep in peace until you come to me.

The stone is hard, and even colder than I thought it would be and it's through to my bones and the marrow in them. I can feel my hip bones, so that's one in the eye for Norah, I have got bones so. I wish I'd never called her Mum. And my elbows ache already, where they're turned out to let my hands lie flat and dead. But I don't care, they're fat little elbows and ugly hands. Anthony's were beautiful. Heart breaking fingers curled over the white satin in the coffin. Long dark eyelashes on wafer-thin skin. Beautiful. Not a great lump. A great big lump. Sometimes I can't remember what it was like to be touched or held or hugged. Sometimes I think maybe I never was held or hugged or loved. Yes, I was. I was. I was. Shut the fuck up, Cheyenne Bodie, what do you know? I was. Bugger. It won't stop.

If I was ten, which I am, and I had never been held or loved, I would have died of it by now. You cannot live to ten without a lick of love and holding. So I must have been. Shut up. Romulus and Remus were brought up by wolves – that's what made me think of 'lick'. They must have been licked.

Your brain can get tired of thinking. Let me die now. Let my heart stop and my brain die and my kidneys turn to stone. Bring Anthony back. Bring him back. Put him in his Mummy's arms and let Norah look down at him and mend everything in that house. Make it right where it's wrong and good where it's bad, because you can do that. You can do everything so why not? You can lift up Lucy Gannon with just a thought and float her away, through wind and weather and clouds and sky to her mother with the rosy cheeks and the shiny black hair and fat little ears like no one else.

And nothing happens and nothing happens. And nothing bloody well happens. For bloody hours on end.

I want to wee. I get up, stiff, and sit in a pew. The door's locked and I'm bone cold but I'm no nearer dying. It must be at least midnight. I look at Christ bleeding on the cross and I say I'm just eight. Nine. I'm only a little girl. Ten. How can I bloody well be expected to do this all on my own? The baby should have lived. That's how it should have been. Happy ever after. A shining little family.

I'm tired and fed up and the swearing's getting worse and I keep seeing that rice pudding and this isn't working and it isn't going to and now I'm locked in the buggering church and I'll be in such trouble. They'll find me, in a pool of wee tomorrow morning, nowhere near dead. My place in the world has gone. Cheyenne has a daughter of his own in California and Danny Boy is as dead as Mammy, and I look at the sacristy lamp and I don't bloody care whether he's here or not. Jesus in the tabernacle. What use is Jesus in a lump of mouldy bread locked away in a stupid tabernacle? That filum was rubbish and he's not going to come down off that cross no matter what, and there's no one to fold me about with their angel wings and guard me and warm me with angel kisses and it doesn't matter what I do or think or swear or anything because I'm just a speck of dust and nothing at all. I don't even like the stupid bloody saints any more. If I was that boy in the *Lord of the Flies* I'd pull off every bloody wing and eat the damn things, for spite, so I would. Which I've never read. Stop it.

Just bloody shut it. Make me. I feel dizzy. My belly aches from holding in the wee. If I just had hold of Jesus now.

Cliff has a house in Spain and Bobby Vee's a big fat girl's blouse and I hate them all. Dear God, I am so full of spite and rage and wanting.

I can hear someone shouting. Bugger and bollocks and shit and bugger and fuck and tarty cow. And crying. Wailing. And a slammed door miles off and running feet. And I can taste salt and honey, a bit like snot and I'm fighting to breathe with all the air sucked out of the space around me. And the shouting goes on, a fury in it, fit to murder. There's a great slab of yellow light and I screw my eyes up against the glare, and gasp for breath and the shouting stops and I realise it was my voice all the time. And then Father Sullivan is looking down at me and the housekeeper comes running behind him, and he puts a hand out to stop her and he says 'Lucy.' And I start to cry softer and he says 'Ah, Lucy, love.' And I say 'I need the loo, I'm desperate.'

We have tea with condensed milk in the presbytery and the housekeeper says I'm a silly girl and Father Sullivan says I'm missing my Mammy and the housekeeper gives me a piece of cake with dry edges and the cream's a bit off but I eat it anyway, starving. It's lovely hearing Father Sullivan say Mammy. No one's said Mammy since I left Aunty Nelly's house and the word makes my eyes prickle and the world goes misty.

There isn't a roaring fire, just an electric one with one bar on and one broken, and a radio and a pile of books and a crossword half-done. It isn't midnight after all, it's barely half past eight, and Father Sullivan puts an old grey cardigan around me and walks me home. We stand outside looking at the flickering light from the telly in the front room. I say 'What's My Line?' and he smiles and nods and then says God won't let the baby come back to life if I die, and even if he did, my Dad would be very upset. And he'd be upset too, he says. And my teachers and all my friends. There would be a lot of crying and carrying on. It would be the funeral of the year. I try not to be happy about this, but I am. He says my brothers would be beside themselves with grief. I think he means beside each other. I say Peter wouldn't and he says 'You'd be surprised.'

He doesn't know Peter.

He says I have to promise I won't go trying to die again and I promise. We look at each other for a long time and then we smile. I think he's finished and I wonder if I should say 'thank you for having me' but he says, all sudden and jerky, 'What do you think God made you for, Lucy?' And I say, because I know my catechism, and I say it sing-song like at school

'God made me to know him, love him, and serve him in this world, and to be happy with him for ever in the next.' And I think he's going to say 'Well, aren't you the great girl?' Because I know it's right, that catechism answer, but he doesn't, he just looks sad and says 'No. God made you because he loves you.' I don't know what to say so I just go 'Oh. Right.'

He says, and it's like Mammy in Scarborough, through his teeth, all wizened up strangled words, 'Forget bloody Purgatory. There is no Purgatory.'

Well. I just look at him. And he rubs his forehead, like there's some impossible sum he has to do. Long division probably. And none of it makes sense. And him, a priest. I wait a bit, so it gets a chance to sort itself out in his head and then in mine but it doesn't. And then he grins a sad sort of grin.

He says they made it up, to get money, the buggers. In the olden days all the cardinals got together in Rome and they made up Purgatory so people would pay not to go there. Or something.

I think he's got that wrong. But he says he hasn't. He says when you've lost someone you love you'd give your eye teeth to get them out of suffering, wouldn't you? I don't know what eye teeth are, but I nod. He says 'Well, then, all the rich people gave their money to the church and that's why we have Purgatory.' So, we stand there a bit longer and I'm not sure what to do now.

He takes the old grey cardigan and touches my shoulder and makes a shush sign and I nod.

And I shall hear, tho' soft you tread above me,
And all my dreams will warm and sweeter be,
If you'll not fail to tell me that you love me,
I'll simply sleep in peace until you come to me.

I let myself into the house and slip up the stairs on Injun moccasin feet, with my black velvet hair cascading down my back and feathers in my head band. Cheyenne's on the landing, and I make an 'enemies below' sign to him and he nods. I close my bedroom door very very quietly.

They made it up. The big fat Catholic fuckers.

CIVVY STREET

The amazing news is that Dad's leaving the Army. He's on leave now and doesn't have to go back so we're going into a new house tomorrow. It's all very exciting and he's got this letter from someone in Buckingham Palace, but not the Queen. Dad's going to be a civilian servant who don't wear bowler hats any more or actually be servants, they just run the country for the government. So it's another goodbye to the teachers and another goodbye to my best friend who is a girl called Louise and her Dad's a Jehovah's Witness which makes my Dad say some people will believe any damn nonsense, when I know for a fact he believes in fairies. Louise cries and I don't know what to say so I tell her 'There was a mad lady of Wopping, who grew very cross while out shopping, she started to cough and her left leg flew off and now she's not mad, she's just hopping,' and she laughs, so that's OK.

I wake up late and the removers are already loading the big van and I have to keep out from under their feet and make myself scarce. Which is hard when there's no chair to sit on and your bed has been taken away and it's raining.

The new house is pebble dash and it's in Orchard Crescent, Chippenham, where there isn't any Orchard, and a weather forecast man used to live here. My room is lilac again, but we didn't paint it. I don't know why it's always bloody lilac. There's three bedrooms so the boys can have the third one when they come on leave. Peter's been in the Navy nearly a year and he hasn't had leave even once but Dad says he has, he's just not bothered coming to see us.

I have a little table for a desk in the dining room and we've not even started unpacking the boxes and had a cup of tea, when there's a knock on the door and a lady called Mrs Pointer is there, with a book of sums and she's going to cram my head with stuff for the Eleven Plus. Dad tells her I'm not stupid, which is not what he usually says, but he says that I'm perverse, which is what Mum usually says.

I'm going to go to school in Chippenham for a bit and then it'll be the convent. It turns out I can go there even if I don't pass my Eleven Plus because we're Roman Catholic and I can go for free but the uniform costs a bloody arm and a leg so get your head down and make the most of this wonderful opportunity. Dad says that will be my tenth school. I only remember four. Five. A few.

And another funny thing, peculiar not ha-ha, is that my birthday is December 2nd. Daddy sent off for my birth certificate because the convent wanted to know and guess what, I've been having a birthday on the wrong day for years. Daddy says it might be something to do with what was in Mammy's head, not a conker, but something I can never remember because it's a terrible thing to say and Aunty Nelly never said it out loud, just moved her mouth. Anyway, either with the conker in her head, or with Dad forgetting, my birthday has been on the wrong day in years.

The school in Chippenham is behind the church and the head mistress says we can go to Benediction every Wednesday after school which is my favourite thing ever. The bell and the monstrance and the incense and all that adoration and genuflecting and it means I'll get home late so it'll already be tea time and I won't have to sit straight down and do a page of long division which I can't do. Sometimes I can't quite remember which school I'm in and when I was in Warminster reading *Children Of The New Forest*, the bit about skinning the deer, the bell went and I stood up, with the book in my hand to finish that page. I thought I was in Golborne and I turned right instead of left, and smacked my nose on the blackboard and it bled so much they couldn't stop it and Dad said was I bloody stupid?

I looked at the sticky blood, smelling like the chains on the swings in the park, and wondered if I was oozing life like Mac the Knife but then it stopped and I had to suck on a piece of ice to make sure it didn't start again and it didn't.

The new new school is in a big old building with stone steps and you can't see out of the windows. I got lost yesterday between the cloakroom and the dinner hall and the teachers were aggravated because they thought I was being difficult or I'd been kidnapped or something, but it doesn't matter. If I swear a bit and things happen like getting in a fight by accident, or that dustbin catching fire, I'll soon be gone so not to worry. The others say I talk funny, but I don't. They do. In the Warminster school I talked Golborne and they talked Moonraker, but Father Sullivan said so what, he talked Mayo but he managed to make himself understood, just about. I'm going to miss him. This lot talk Moonraker too but they think they're it. Daddy told them about me not talking at all some days and the teacher said they'd soon put a stop to that and there will be so much going on I won't have time to be quiet. Which doesn't make any sense at all. You don't have to have time to be quiet. You can be quiet with no time at all. I don't mean that. I mean something else but anyway.

We do this test to see if we're ready to do the Eleven Plus and because it's my first week they'll make allowances. The next day the teacher talks to Mum and I've distinguished myself by getting the lowest marks ever in Arithmetic. Mum says. 'You've distinguished yourself, so well done.' Dad doesn't even look at me. It's hard for him because he's an Army Chess champion and he keeps getting prizes from the *Telegraph* crossword people and he trained as a priest until the war started. Having a daughter like me. He knows Latin better than old Canon Castledine and when they had a Latin poem for a funeral he told them what it was in English because they didn't know. All they know is church Latin, which he says is bastardised which is not a bad word, unless you shout it at someone. Once, when Canon Castledine was in the pulpit he said 'Tempus Fewjit' and Daddy said 'Fug-it' and everyone looked at us. And he does Greek and went to Welsh seminary where they never spoke to him in English so he had no choice but to learn Welsh so he says poems in it and no one knows what he's on about. Anyway, Mum says it makes me a bit of an anomaly. I don't know what that is. One of the Welsh poems is about a fox on a wall and Dad says it doesn't matter what the words mean, just listen to the melody. I say it's all Greek to me, which is a good joke, and he smiles and says the old ones are the best.

And we have a car! It's a blue Standard 8 Companion and it has red seats and Dad is a really terrible driver. That's what Norman says. Norman gave Dad his first lesson and afterwards he polished off all Daddy's birthday whisky for shock. Daddy said it would have been cheaper to buy the bloody driving school. Dad buggers and panics when it kangaroo hops, but Norman swears really terrible swears. I'm not to tell Mum about the swearing or she won't let me come again and at least it gets me out from under her feet because she can't think with me there, forever getting in the way. Last week I was in the back seat, sort of day dreaming and sleepy, and we suddenly did a kangaroo hop and Norman sucked in his breath and Dad swore a bad word he usually never swears and the engine stopped. So I looked up. And we were half way over a big road with lots of cars and lorries and things, loads of them, and we were stuck sort of sideways in the middle, and there was a car coming towards us on my side and another car coming towards us on Dad's side and Norman said, all squeaky and loud 'Don't panic, they've seen you.' And Daddy swore again and did something to the engine and we hopped a bit and stopped again and Norman said 'Fuck a fucking brick – shit – bugger.' which is really quite bad even for Norman. And Dad did something else to the engine and we hopped once, twice, and the car on my side did a swerve around us, blowing its horn like mad, and it shook the whole car it went so close – and now we were right in front of another car coming the other way and it was big and black and I looked at Dad in the mirror and he had his eyes shut. Norman shouted this big loud shout 'Fuck me – ignition on, clutch in… you can do this.' But Dad made a sort of puppy noise and put his head on the wheel and whoosh! the black car was past us and now a lorry was coming and I could see the driver and he had his mouth open and he was sort of standing up behind his steering wheel and his lorry went a bit sideways and there was this crunch moment when you duck down even though it isn't going to help and you hold your breath even though that won't help – then the lorry stopped and we could hear the engine clanking and we sat there in silence for a minute and you could feel lumps of dust falling down in the air, and everything was cold. My neck was wet and I don't know why. So was Dad's.

Then Norman said, all gentle and fierce at the same time, 'Get the fuck out of that fucking seat you bloody fucking eedjit' and Dad got out and Norman swished across and Dad walked round and got into Norman's seat and Norman waved 'sorry' to everyone and we moved on, across the road. No one said anything for ages.

Then Norman said 'Sorry about the language, Luce' and I said 'It's OK.'

But the good thing, the really good good thing and a huge wonderful thing is that Father Sullivan is in Chippenham too! We went to Mass the second Sunday after moving and sat in a pew with a brass thing on it 'A Gift From The Polish People' and Dad said that was very thoughtful of Kiwi and I laughed and he was surprised and asked if I knew what a pun was and I said I did and he was surprised all over again. And then I looked up and it was Father Sullivan coming in swinging the censer, and I was really happy and Daddy groaned.

THE CASE OF THE
POISONED FISHKNIFE

Today I'm exactly ten and a half. No one knows but me. Daddy takes me into Chippenham to a meeting for soldiers who left the Army and we watch *Tomorrow We Live*, and I'm the only child there but Norah needs a break and some time to grieve without... but Dad doesn't say without what, just pulls a face so I stay and watch it and it's the best film ever. Dad says it's proper grander and a waste of time and effort and are we all bloody children? On the way home, which we have to walk because Norman says Dad isn't ready for his driving test yet and may not be until the age of miracles comes upon us, I am a beautiful girl in the French Resistance and my name is Lulu LaBelle. Douglas Bader is my Dad. Or he may be my sweetheart, I haven't made up my mind. I'll have to see. I still truly love Cheyenne Bodie and I've found out all sorts of things about Clint Walker who is the actor, because Aunty Nelly sent me a magazine with him in it and Mum sniffed but Dad said 'For God's sake, it'll keep her quiet' so I read it over and over. I think I may love him with all my heart which means that we are fated to be together although the world may conspire against us. Which it's doing so far with me being ten and him being grown up, not just Clint but all of them; Perry Como, Cliff and Marty Wilde and Maigret, Harry Secombe, Perry Mason, Bobby Vee, Anne Frank and all the Cartwrights off the Ponderosa. And Nancy Spain. Nancy is very cheeky on *Twenty Questions*, and would be as good in a tight corner, like George from *The Famous Five*. But then you think too much, like when I'm on my cayuse in the Rockies with Anne Frank and I suddenly think 'How does she know how to ride, with being hidden in a cupboard for the whole war?' And the whole thing's ruined and I'm back in the lilac room, or doing the washing up or whatever I was doing. When it works, this thing in my head, it's lovely but when it doesn't it's aggravating and sometimes people have seen me talking and they can't see Elvis or anyone so they think I'm loopy. Which I'm not.

A cayuse is a pony. I asked Mrs Holmes at school and she didn't know but the next day she told me she'd looked it up. She asked me what I'm reading and I say *Rebecca* and she says it's wrong to lie and no one's impressed. So I say *The Famous Five* and she smiles and says that's better. But Dad says Enid Blyton's as bad as yankee pap so I can only read it when I go to someone's house for tea. Which is rude so sometimes I steal the book and read it in bed and give it back later, and they think I took it by mistake. It doesn't matter what I read anyway because as soon as I've read it, I forget it, with my brain. Sometimes I read a book twice and only realise when it's nearly finished.

There's a new regiment today in the new house. New house, new school, new regiment, Dad keeps saying how much better it is than everything we had before but I can't keep up. The new regiment is that I have my tea as soon as I get in, sitting at the table alone but with the table set for Dad and Mum for their dinner, later. Today, the first day of the new plan, I change my shoes and wash my hands upstairs and put my school uniform on the chair and change into a skirt and jumper and come down. I'm not sure what to do now because the to-do list just says 'Tea'. I haven't seen Mum yet and I can hear her in the kitchen but I'm not sure if I'm allowed in. I sneak a quick look in the dining room and there it is, set out. There's a boiled egg and a piece of bread and butter, and next to it an apple and a glass of Kia Ora which means good health in Maori. Mum lived in New Zealand for years so she should know. I sit down and eat my egg and look at the places set for Mum and Dad and they have fish knives and if they're going to have that slimy-skin fish they're welcome. Mum got the knives for Christmas, and they came in a box with a red velvet inside which is beautiful. Dad said 'How posh' and Mum said it's not posh to say posh.

The next bit of the regiment is that I pile up my crocks neatly and get on with Mrs Pointer's homework at my desk, here in the dining room. It's long division again, and the numbers are millions long with o's which are called noughts and a nought means nothing but then sometimes it can mean ten or a hundred or a thousand and it can go right up to a million billion if there are lots of them. But lots of nothing is nothing so it's just nonsense and you'd think someone would sort it out really. I pick up the resistance story where I left it, in a cellar, telling the Nazis I'll never talk. I haven't talked since I got home nearly two hours ago so I've had lots of practice.

By the time Dad gets in, my back is whipped red raw and the SS Major says Lancashire girls are a breed apart like Gracie Fields, and the sums haven't done themselves. Dad goes into the kitchen first and I can hear them laughing and talking and Dad sings some song I don't know and Mum calls out 'Ten minutes' as he goes into the sitting room to put the news on. Ten minutes. I make a start on the sums.

People see us everywhere
They think you really care,
But myself, I can't deceive,
I know it's only make believe

When Mum carries their dinner through she says all bright and friendly 'There we are, Lucy, I'm out of your way so you can get on with your washing up' and she's saying it so Dad will hear but we both pretend she isn't. It's the first thing she's said to me and she still hasn't looked at me. When I pass her in the doorway, taking my eggshell and stuff, Dad squeezes past and he smiles and says 'Alright, Lucy Lastic?' And I say yes and go through to the sink. So I have talked. But I didn't tell them anything even though they pulled my fingernails out.

As I run the hot water for the fishy pan I look at myself in the window and pull a horrible face. Sometimes I talk to Anthony and tell him he's well out of it but I know that's not true. If he was here it would all be different. And anyway, he's a baby and babies can't understand. I'm just finishing the drying and I'm running the hot water again for their plates when Mum brings them through. Dad's gone in to watch And The Next Tonight Will Be Tomorrow Night and I hear the music which is happy things-to-do music. She doesn't say anything. And then the silence is like a big wall and we can't pretend it's not happening so she has to think of something to say and I can't make it easy for her because I can't stop her not liking me. I wish I could because it's not her fault Anthony died and I don't think she'll ever bounce back. Ever. She says 'How was school?' and it's like one of my Nazis is at her throat with a bayonet and she hates betraying the underground cell, but she's had the truth drug and she just can't help it. A sort of strangled 'How was school?', Not a tell-me-everything sort of thing at all. So I say 'Wonderful' and she smiles at the wall and goes into the front room with Daddy. At least she hasn't asked about my bloody bowels.

My only prayer will be,
Some day you'll care for me,
But it's only make believe
My hopes, my dreams come true
My life, I'd give for you
But it's only make believe.

It's eight o clock and I'm in bed and it's still light and I can hear the little twins opposite playing tag. I could read till it gets too dark, but I've finished *Rebecca*. The only other book up here is *Lives of The Saints*. Mum gave it to me for my birthday. I like it because the pages are very thin and the edges are gold and the cover is leather, which makes it look very holy. So I get it down from the bookshelf and flick through and find Saint Lucy. I think she must have looked like Sophia Loren who is on the front of the magazines in the papershop, because a boy said they were nice eyes and she didn't want to be vain so she gouged them out. Just like that. It says she's a martyr so she must have bled to death. Like my nose bleed when I walked into the blackboard but infinitely worse. I find Saint Ignatius of Loyola, another good one. He used this scourge to do penance, slicing into his flesh with relish. At first I thought he must have rubbed it in, but then I realised it's the other sort of relish. If he'd rubbed real relish in he'd have gone lunatic with the pain.

I wonder if I could scourge my back for my Mammy instead of saying the Rosary. Or something like that. So I dig my nails into my arm really hard, the white bit of my arm where it's all soft. And I keep digging them in dead hard and when I look there are four little crescent shapes so I offer them to Saint Theresa and ask her to pass them on to the BVM to her son. But not for her son, for Mammy. I say another prayer to make that absolutely clear and apologise for the confusion. The Protties go straight to God. Which is a proud and bold thing to do, which the nuns said when the Protties threw stones at us in Omagh. Years and years and eons ago, when I had a Mammy. It's getting dark at last.

I snuggle down and close my eyes ... Perry Mason ... and that Della one...... The Case of the Poisoned Fish Knife.

THE SHEEP FROM
THE GOATS

The alarm's gone off and I can hear Dad downstairs and I'm putting my socks on when Mum comes to the door and makes me jump. She's all tight and bright and smiley and she says it's the Eleven Plus today, the first part of it, which I didn't know. Yesterday it was bloody weeks off and time to cram which is a thing for thick people, and now here it is. Daddy comes half way up the stairs on his way to the Civil Service, which is not the civilian service like I thought, and says 'Good Luck' and 'Do Your Best' and I say I will. He starts to go down the stairs but he stops and says 'How are you getting on with Mum?' And I say 'Good.' And he says 'Yes?' And I say 'Yes' while in my head I'm saying 'You must be bloody blind and buggering deaf.' But I don't say it out loud so he nods and goes down the stairs to catch the bus, walking past the egg blue car that cost two hundred quid and will never get used at this rate.

I make sure my bedroom door is closed and then say bugger it, quite loud.

I've got a plaster on my arm where the little moon marks have gone yellow and Mum washes them in TCP which stings like torture. I read this story about Padre Pio who has the stigmata and when my arm started going red and sore I thought maybe my half moons were stigmata and I forgot that I made them with my nails. So I told Father Kennedy in confession and said that there was no sign of nail holes in my hands and feet yet but I'd not given up hope and he said 'Dear Jesus, bloody hell.' but not smiley like Father Sullivan. Dad says he takes a bottle of whisky, a hot water bottle and the *Racing Times* into the confessional.

Mum tells me to do my best, which I will, and gives me a little tiny crucifix just to borrow for the exam room, which is the hall. She wasn't born Catholic, she converted when she was twenty-eight. Dad says the converts are the worse and I think he's sort of joking but not really. She said it sorts the sheep from the goats, the Eleven Plus, and he said she knows her Bible backwards. Which she doesn't.

It's the English exam, which I finish before everyone else and the teacher who has curly hairs up his nose says have I checked my answers but I have. He shakes his head at me like I'm lying and says I can read it through one more time and everyone looks at me. I say I've read it through twice and he says I can fold my arms then and wait, like I've done something wrong and he's telling me off. Perry Mason is at the desk at the front of the hall and he raises his eyebrows and we both know he could devastate hairy nose in two minutes with his cross questioning and that stare. Then we have playtime and two of the teachers I don't know are looking at me and talking so I wonder what I've done. The next test is comprehension and it's a bit of 'You Are Old Father William' from Dad's bloody Alice books and I finish first again. To stop the teacher with the nose hairs carrying on like before, I write out the rest of the poem, which is very long, and I say it's in *Alice In Wonderland* by Lewis Carroll which I don't like but I know some people do, and horses for courses. I have to ask for another piece of paper and I get another funny look.

Anything you can do, I can do better, I can do anything better than you.

The next day it's the Arithmetic test and I finish first again. But I don't need any extra paper because I only answer two questions and they are guesses. But I know what to do this time, I fold my arms and choose a name for my *Swallows and Amazons* boat, and then a colour, and then a picnic we can take on our adventure and then I work out our adventure. Me and Adam Faith and Elvis and we fill that little boat but we balance it out nicely, Adam at the front, Elvis at the back and me in the middle. And then it's playtime again. The Problem Test is dead easy – mixed up words and odd words out. There's a question about numbers, which absolutely isn't fair but I skip that one. And we have to write a paragraph but I write a page and it's brilliant, I write and write and write and it goes onto another page and the only bad thing is that the exam is over before my writing is. So Hairy Nose winks and says I can have another ten minutes but don't tell anyone on pain of death. And I finish as he gathers up the pages and cleans the blackboard.

Anything you can be I can be greater. Sooner or later, I'm greater than you.

We start Confirmation Classes and thanks to the *Lives Of The Saints* I have my names all picked out. My name now is Lucy Mary and when the Bishop comes I'll be Lucy Mary Theresa Frances Bernadette. Everyone's going to be Theresa because there's a huge picture of her in our class and she's got lovely long eyelashes. I'd like Ignatius too but Father Sullivan says enough's as good as a feast and he has his doubts about that gentleman. Father Sullivan isn't as shy as he was. He still 'Dearly Beloved Brethren's every five minutes but he doesn't close his eyes and sweat any more. Everyone was surprised when he came to the

Confirmation class and told them all that we were old friends. Penny Wright whispered 'Teacher's pet' and I said pot and kettle, which was very quick and she didn't know what to say. I'm not sure what it means.

My exam results come before everyone else's and I have to go and talk to someone in the County Council and he's a doctor but he's the sort who'd be useless if you took a broken leg to him. I have the highest marks in English and no marks at all in Arithmetic and they think maybe I wasn't well that day, but the teachers have written to say I'm always like that and the doctor says it's how I am. I'm an enigma as well as an anomaly. He asks me what I think I'm good at and I say everything really, especially singing.

Anything you can sing I can sing sweeter.
I can sing anything sweeter than you.

Which is not absolutely true. Which is different from saying 'Which is absolutely not true.' and it means I am quite good at singing but not absolutely grand.

The doctor tells Daddy that I have moved house eleven times in my life and three times in the last year and it's made me unstabled. Like a horse. It wasn't unstabled but something like unstabled came into it. Dad says not three times in a year, three times in 18 months and the doctor says 'And she's lost everyone who mattered to her, her mother, her aunty, her brothers' and Dad stands up, quick-sticks and the chair scrapes and he says 'Not everyone.' And we leave.

Mum says subnormal is a terrible word and we shouldn't use it. I didn't know we ever did.

They keep talking about me, and sometimes Daddy looks at me for a long time when he thinks I've not noticed. If I look at him, he looks away. I think my grey matter is really gone now. I can't remember my Mammy, but I want her all the time, every waking minute.

Which is also absolutely not true and bonkers but it's how I feel sometimes even though the next minute I'm in Berlin killing Hitler, happy as Larry. If I was an animal I'd be a ravening wolf and I'd track her down, even over snow and rivers, even though I know she's dead and not in the world at all. I can't remember how old I was when she died or the smell of her or anything. I had a dunlopillow that she slept with and it smelt of her for ages but the smell went and Aunty Nelly said it was time to give it a Christian burial, which we didn't. It went on the rubbish cart.

I want to kill Mum and I want her to say she's sorry and I want her to love me, along with us all being happy ever after and Anthony coming back to life but I know none of that can happen, especially not the killing Mum bit. Someone like Perry Mason could get me off but I'd always be looking over my shoulder like a fugitive from justice. Which I would be. I want to kill Daddy too but he's trained Infantry so it would be hand to hand combat and bayonets, and it could go on for days, over-turning furniture and throttling each other and mayhem. Mum would be dead easy, a knife in her eyeball through to her brain.

I'm so tired with that horse waking me up all the time and no one can tell me what happens to graves and I've run out of people to ask. I can't do bloody sums and the simplest things are lumps of cotton wool in my brain and sometimes I forget where I live. I told the school nurse I live in Melksham but I've never even been there, just heard Dad talk about it. Even the thoughts I think are sins so I can't do right for doing wrong. If Father Sullivan's got the wrong end of the stick and there is a Purgatory after all, I'm going to be there bloody centuries at this rate and there won't be any one to get me out, either. Unless me and Clint are married and then he can grieve for me and pay for some Masses, being very rich and living in California. But he's already thirty years older than me so God knows how much older than me he'll be when I die. Hundreds of years.

I may have come first in writing my stupid essay but that won't help if I end up in a hospital for people with mad brains, and I won't be able to fight them off when they come for me, the men in white coats. When they took my Aunty Lucy off to Winwick Asylum she didn't want to go and she cried and tried to bite the men, but they took her anyway, for her own good. It was just after she gave Peter and me big glasses of yellow custard stuff with brandy in it and eggs. Peter was sick all down the post box, bright yellow sick on the red and black paint and I was sick all down Peter. And then Aunty Lucy said something rude to the doctor and started to kiss him and take her dress off and they took her away. I was named after her, which Uncle Alf said was asking for trouble.

I empty my money box, two pounds thirteen and seven pence and I walk to the train station instead of school. A train to London, that's top of my to-do list. And number two is a train to Wigan. Number three is a walk to Golborne. Number four is throw open the scullery door, 'Ey up, Aunty Nelly! It's me!'

FREE PASSAGE

I'm not absolutely positively certain where the train station is but the path to school is just beside the railway so I'll just follow it, like Hiawatha following the river. With a name like that he ought to be a girl and I thought he was for ages so when I read this poem I had to keep going back over it. I usually leave the house at half eight so I get to school with a little bit of playtime but today I leave early, so I'll miss everyone.

In case anyone stops me I've written a letter, and copied Dad's signature.

Dear whoever reads it, Lucy is on a mission to Lancashire. Due to the official secrets act I am not at liberty to say any more and she must pass by unhindered. Signed Gerard Gannon, CSM, Royal Inniskilling Fusiliers.

I like the unhindered bit. It's something the Queen would say. And they won't know he's left the Army.

I walk onto the main road and down Sheldon Road where Mary Lord, my friend, lives. Even though I'm so early she's sitting on the step waiting for me and I say 'Bum' but quietly and wonder what to do now. But she's seen me and she waves so I wave back. Should I tell her? She won't understand because she has a Mammy and a Daddy and he does tricks with thrupenny pieces and makes them come out of our ears and we all laugh like we're daft babies.

But he's nice and so is her Mammy who has breasts you can't stop looking at and I want to squeeze them to see what they feel like but it would be shameful. We walk on, and I've taught her how to march so we go in step, past the Bird's Eye place where Mum might get a job when her insides have mended from Anthony, and then we're at the crossroads and the station is one way and the school is the other. So I say 'Platoon, platoon shun.' and grab Mary and I tell her something terrible happened to Aunty Nelly. Her mouth is always open because she has adenoids so I look at her tongue as I tell her because it's hard lying when you look into someone's eyes. And I say 'My Aunty has scrofula and is dying and has asked for me before it's too late.' And Mary says 'Is that the Aunty married to Max Bygraves?' And for a minute I can't remember who's married to who, then I say yes, but he's broken his leg so he can't look after her. And bloody Mary starts crying for Aunty Nelly. And then for Max. There in the street. Bloody crying. I tell her to shut up but she's bawling with long strings of spit so I give her a bit of a shove and she hiccup-talks so it's hard to understand but I think she says it's an awful thing, scrofula, like eczema but worse. And poor Max, in plaster. I didn't know scrofula was like eczema, I thought it was dropsy and she says 'No, that's leprosy' and lets out another bloody big bawl. The whole thing's so sad I feel the tears coming and the lump in my throat to keep her company.

Now everyone's looking and wouldn't you know, Hairy Nose stops in a little green car with wood on it and says 'What's going on, girls?' And bloody Mary says 'Her aunty has the scrofula and Max Bygraves has a broken leg so she has to be there to let the priest in for the last rites.' I didn't say anything about the last bloody rites. She's gone too far. I say quick sticks 'Aunty Nelly may not be dying – she may just be in extremis.' And Hairy Nose raises his eyebrows and tells us to stop buggering about and get into school. So we do.

I've got two pounds, thirteen and seven pence in my pocket. I could ask Mrs Gordon to look after it but then she'll ask all sorts of questions, so I put it in my shoe and get a blister.

On the way home we go to the Home & Colonial with my money and Mary has a Crunchie and I have a Bounty. She says she's sorry about stopping me going to Golborne. It's the first Bounty I've had since I left Aunty Nelly's and it's better than anything. Sweets are unnecessary and banned from the house because I'm such a fat little thing but when I said this to Mary's Mammy on my birthday she said 'You're bonny, love.' So I told Mum and she was really cross and said that saying bonny was just another way of saying 'fat' and I shouldn't talk about what happens at home anyway. Which I didn't even know. I know it about Golborne, I didn't know it about here. Maybe it's about everywhere.

This is the first time in all that time that I've done anything, anything anything anything, that I'm not allowed to do and it's lovely and exciting and I feel like *Just William* who I read last week and it made me laugh. Before Dad married Mum I could do a million things I wasn't allowed to and no one ever knew and if they did, so what. Now, with the to-do list and not upsetting Norah and all of that, all I'm allowed to do is breathe. Just.

When I get home, Mum is pink and happy and excited and she comes out of the kitchen and I'm so surprised I just stand there. She's pretty again. She's got a job in the Home & Colonial! It's like my belly hits my bum. If I was wearing a corset like Queen Victoria had to, I'd probably swoon. Mum says 'What's wrong?' And I say 'Nothing.' and go through to my boiled egg and Kia Ora. Just thinking about it makes my insides go to jelly. If she'd started work today and I'd gone in with my sock full of money...

and Mary..... or if I'd already bought the Crunchie and Bounty and turned round and walked slap bang into her! So before I get into bed I make a little shrine to Saint Nicholas, the patron saint of thieves and I put the rest of my money back in its little box. I know I'm not a thief because it was my money but I feel like one.

I clean my teeth extra well to make up for the Bounty and keep doing it till my mouth bleeds again and I offer that up. I'll still have to confess it, because it feels like a sin, and I didn't tell Mum what I did which I think is probably a Sin Of Omission, but I'll explain to the priest that I've already done the penance. Bleeding mouth. But if it's Father Kennedy who is not a nice priest but a fierce one, he might tell Daddy because although they go on about how your secrets are safe in confession and a priest would rather die than tell them, it's all fat lies. At my first ever confession in Golborne I told Canon Castledine that Uncle Alf hurt me in the night and hit Peter and Canon Castledine said I should be ashamed of myself for barefaced lying like that.

When I got home after going up the slag heap with everyone, the bloody bastard priest was just leaving and I got the belting of my life and so did Peter. Peter didn't know what he was being lathered for, but he sort of knew it was me that did it and he called me a bitch. Which is worse than a bastard.

The belting of my life. And Uncle Alf told Nelly I'd took his beer money and she knew it wasn't true but she said 'There's no need to beat the daylights out of her.' And she didn't even ask why Peter got the thrashing. Because she knew really.

I'll never tell a priest anything secret again, so I won't. The next time I had to go to Confession I walked all the way to Newton Le Willows, which took half a lifetime, and confessed my sins there in the church where Mammy's buried so the priest wouldn't know me at all. Mary and Saint John's church in Newton Le

Willows is a big cold old place and I think there may be ghosts lurking, and scarey, but I did it. I just told him about swearing and sulking and maybe other stuff, I can't remember. My penance was four Our Fathers which are a lot more uncomfortable to the tongue than Hail Marys but at least there was no way my sins were going to be slathered all over Golborne. Then, as I got up to go, this priest – I don't know who it was – said to me, bold as brass 'And how's your Daddy doing, Lucy love?'

The good bit about walking all that way was that I went to Mammy's grave, and I sat with her for a bit until my bottom got cold and I was on the brink of varicoses and had to get up. Aunty Frances is buried just two graves away, which is sad and beautiful at the same time. Mary and Frances were sisters and they married two brothers, my Daddy and Uncle Frank. Gerry and Mary travelled all over the world with the Army and Frances and Frank stayed put but the sisters died within a few weeks of each other and were buried just two graves apart. All those years apart and now together for all eternity. Or until the council digs up all the graves. Bugger. Don't start that again. You're just asking for trouble.

Anyway, half past seven and bed. I'm not on a train on my way to Lancashire and I'm not walking up Legh Street and I'm not running down our jitty with my footsteps echoing on the cobbles, and I am definitely not throwing the door open and jumping onto Aunty Nelly's big soft lap and feeling her fat happy arms around me.

My Aunty Nelly, She had a wooden belly, And every time she walked, It wobbled like a jelly.

One day, when I'm older and going to the convent and I'm catching a train every morning, I'll walk down the platform and cross over to the other platform and I'll get on a train going the other way. London is like three Manchesters so no one will know where to start looking. I'll vanish into the crowds and get a job sweeping the streets and when they think I'm dead, I'll go up to Golborne and put my finger to my lips and Aunty Nelly will sneak me in and I'll live in a secret room like Anne Frank and sing myself to sleep every night.

MARY'S DAD

Martin's home for a whole week! He's being posted to Borneo so this is the last we'll see of him for a year so it's sad but a whole week is a long time and he comes to meet me every day from school and he walks with me every morning and I want him to wear his uniform but he says he'll look a right berk, like Bernard Breslaw in *The Army Game*. I say he's a lot more handsome than Bernard Breslaw and he doesn't talk like him either, so Martin promises to wear it on his last day which is next Monday so I say OK.

He arrived on Saturday and he seemed really happy but on Sunday he wasn't so happy and he took Daddy into the garden and I could hear them arguing which we never do with Daddy. Peter used to slam doors but no one ever argues with Daddy. And I walk through the kitchen to see what's wrong but Mum grabs my arm and pulls me back and tells me to go upstairs. I'm always having to go up the bloody stairs. And she says 'Don't look at me like that.' And I think she's going to hit me but I don't know why, but she doesn't. When I go upstairs I don't go into my room and instead I creep into Mum and Dad's room so I can hear what Martin's saying just under the window. He says 'She never looks at her. You're as bad. It's like she's a bloody ghost in her own home. If you can call it a home.' I think he must have seen Mammy's ghost and I get a bit scared so I hurry to my room and I shut the door and I make the sign of the cross.

I'm not afraid of Mammy but I might be a little bit frightened of her ghost, I'm not sure. That night Mammy died, when she came and kissed me and she could see and walk and everything, I think she may have been a ghost then. Aunty Nelly says she wasn't quite dead yet and that was her soul saying goodbye. Peter said it was rubbish, and just a dream but Aunty Nelly said Mammy had been blind for two years, why would I dream that she kissed me on the one night in two years that she died? And she said I was so sure when I came downstairs that morning that everyone knew something had happened. Peter was very angry because he says that Mammy loved him best and when they knew she was dying they should have woken him up. He thinks that if Mammy was going to kiss anyone goodbye it would have been him. I think maybe she did but he just slept through it. Just before she died she said to Martin 'Look after my thorn between two roses.' And that was Peter, and Martin said he would. Then she said 'And what will happen to my little Lucy?' And then she just upped and died. We don't know what will happen to her little Lucy yet, but Peter won't let anyone look after him, no one at all. Daddy calls him 'our thorny problem' but I don't think he remembers what Mammy said, I don't think that's why he says it.

It's the end of Junior school and to celebrate I'm going to tea with Mary. I'm not to let the side down and forget my manners. Her Mammy's made a great load of little cakes and her little sisters have made cards for us and then her big sister Patricia gets out a Dansette, which is a record player, and we listen to 'Smoke Gets In Your Eyes' over and over again. Pat says it was number one which means everyone likes it, but that was ages ago and she's amazed that I haven't heard it. I say I have, which I haven't, obviously. It's very sad. I like sad things. I like happy things too.

Mary tells Pat that we don't have a TV and I've never even

seen *Oh, Boy!* which is a programme about pop music. We do have a TV but I don't say anything because then they'll know that I'm not allowed to watch it except on Friday and Saturday. I think they would look at me funny. Daddy doesn't believe in pop and we have a record player and a record of *A Little Night Music*, which is German, and *Elizabethan Serenade*, which is English, because that's a damn good introduction to proper music. We're saving up for a radiogram. I asked if I could spend some of my money box money on a record but Dad said 'Oh, God, she'll soon be a teenager.' and that was that. He said they never used to have teenagers. You were a child to start with and then a grown up. I don't know how that worked.

In Catechism Father Sullivan said some things are mysteries and we're not supposed to find the answers in this life, maybe the next, but most things we wonder about are just puzzles and if we wait patiently we'll get the answers. I asked about Purgatory and everybody groaned. And Father Sullivan said for pity's sake, are we back on that auld horse and cart? He thought it was back in the stable. And no one knew what he was on about except him and me and I felt sad because maybe he thought that I didn't believe him. And I do. There is no Purgatory. But, just in case. He smiled though so it was OK and said try to forget about Purgatory, just say a decade of the Rosary for Mammy once in a blue moon and get on with being a child. I said Aunty Nelly said the prayers of a child were special but soon I'll be a teenager which is a very modern thing entirely. And I said if the prayers of a teenager weren't the same as them from a child, where did that leave Mammy? and Father Sullivan said 'God, but you're hard work sometimes.' And I asked why God let people be unhappy and he said 'Are you unhappy?' And I said 'No. I have a lovely home and a lovely Mummy and Daddy so why would I be not happy?'

So, all in all, I'm none the wiser. About anything.

Mary's Mam puts a great pile of bread and butter in the middle of the table and we make sausage sandwiches and there's tea with sugar and a big bowl of mash. Everyone talks and the baby shouts and dribbles and it's bonkers. And lovely. She says grace first, like Mum, but she gallops through it and they all shout 'Amen!' and laugh. Mary's Dad says that's them straight to Hell for sure and they don't even listen to him, they just reach across for another sausage or call each other a pig and no one tells them off because they don't mean it. Her Daddy's English and a Protestant but he says he's a don't-know-and-don't-care-much but Mary's Mammy has a Mass said for him every Christmas and he raises merry hell about it and says why can he not get twenty fags and a bottle of whisky like every other Dad? She says she'll drag him into Heaven if it's the last thing she does – which it will be. Obviously.

When Pat brings the cakes in from the kitchen she has to sing all the way so her mam will know she's not eating one of them already. And then we all watch Val Doonican and we're squashed on three big lumpy chairs and the little ones are crawling around our feet and Mary's Dad says there's no bloody comfort at all to be had but no one takes any notice and he puts Mary on his lap and in about two minutes his head is back and he's snoring. Mary's Mum turns the telly up so we can still hear it. I can smell her Dad. He's woodbines and beer and something like chocolate and lovely. I want to stroke his arm which is very hairy but I don't. On Sunday evenings Dad and me watch *Great Expectations* and I love it more than anything I've ever seen or read or even thought about in my whole life. Mum goes into the garden or somewhere and Dad and me don't say a word all through it. Anyway, Mary's Dad is quite like the convict. When the first episode finished I asked Dad if the convict was killed after he was caught on those marshes but he just said 'Wait and see' and winked. It's the first time he's winked for years. Months. And Mary's Dad isn't muddy and fierce but he is bald and big. I would steal a ham and a cake and all sorts for him if he was starving. Here I am sitting next to his big hairy arms and listening to his terrible snore and smelling his fee fi fo fum blood of an Englishman, and it's lovely.

I'm going to ask for *Great Expectations* for Christmas. I could have a library ticket and get two books out every week like Mary does but Mum says there's mumps in books, and the TB germ, so I can't. And maybe it's good that I can't read the book now because then I'd know how the TV programme ended. I've started taking two books at a time from the free pile at the Church and I've usually finished them by Friday and then Saturday's like a great empty desert of nothing and I have to make up stories which are never as surprising as a book written by someone else. Obviously. I wonder why the books at church haven't got the mumps and TB. Maybe it's the holy water. I don't know why it's called *Great Expectations* but I suppose he couldn't call it 'Not Very Great Expectations At All' because then no one would pick it up or make a TV thing about it. If I wrote a book I would call it 'The Amazingly Astonishing Story' so that everyone would buy it, to see if it really was.

The other programme I'm allowed to watch is *Dixon of Dock Green* and I quite like his son-in-law, who's a bit soft right enough. I like some of the criminals too. There aren't any ladies doing great and noble or even clever things on the telly. Most of them are just wives, except for Nancy Spain who tells everyone off and is very funny. But someone should tell the TV people that ladies can be brave and clever too because I saw *Carve Her Name With Pride* that last week in Golborne and the girl in that, Violette, did all sorts of brave things.

I have to leave Mary's at seven, sharp and when I keep check-ing the time Mary's Mum says 'Stop getting in a state, a few minutes won't matter.' but I explain about routine and Mum know-ing where she is and not being at my beck and call and Mary's Mam says 'She needs something to fill her days, that one' but then bites her lip and we all know she's remembered about Anthony and is making allowances which we all have to do all the time for Mum. Then she says she's sure my Mum is a lovely lady. Which she is. And Mary's Daddy says, all high and like it's just a question he's just thought of, but he hasn't, 'And she's nice is she, your step mother?' And I say 'Yes, she's lovely and kind and the best Mummy anyone could ever have.' But it comes out too loud and fierce so I say 'And we laugh all the time.' They all smile and say that's good but they look at each other. I don't know why I said that, except it's how it should be. It's how I want it to be, and it's how Mum wants it to be, and it's how Daddy wants it to be. And it's no one's fault that it's all going wrong. Except maybe me, a little bit, for being so big and stupid. But I'm not stupid in my head. Something happens between my brain and the world and my cleverness gets lost.

And I think maybe it's me. It's not Mum or Mammy dying or Uncle Alf or anything but it's me.

On the walk home me and Violette keep close to the walls, in the shadows, to make sure we're not spotted by the Boche. I have a mac, tied tight in my middle and a beret, and bright red lipstick, just like Violette. You'd think we were twins. I can't really remem-ber much about that Carving film, just that I cried and cried and Aunty Nelly said it was the last bloody time she was taking me to the pictures, which it was. And I had a choc ice.

When I get married I'll pick someone like Mary's Dad. A man with hairy arms. Perry Mason. Or Clint Walker. Not Cliff. And when I get married I'll have a lovely full-up house and we'll have nappies drying by the fire and toys will be scattered all over and my husband will step on them and swear terrible swear words, and we'll just laugh.

We get to the end of Sheldon Road but there's a German tank parked by the lights and a blond officer with a scar all the way from his hair, down through his eyelids and over his cheek to his mouth, which is puckered up in a cruel sneer. Violette makes a gasp and stops dead and I can see she doesn't know what to do next. It's all up to me now. There are four British airmen holed up in the egg farm, and one of us has to take them to the secret air-field. It's a small price to pay for the freedom of France and the end of the war so I put my hands on my hips and walk across the road, dead slow. On tip toe because of my bright red shiny high heels. In the middle I stop and take out a cigarette and light it, like I have all the time in the world. I take this big puff and purse my lips and blow smoke towards the officer and he goes all still. It's a Moment Frozen in Time. He starts to walk across to me. He can't take his eyes off me. I look him up and down, sort of insolent, and then I look away, like I'm bored, and Violette runs behind him, unnoticed and vanishes up the council estate. She'll soon be sorting out the landing lights for the RAF lads and the rescue plane. As he comes close, the German smiles, a slow and lazy smile, almost handsome if you don't mind a scar or two. And then a big Bird's Eye lorry hoots its horn dead loud and I nearly wet myself. The driver leans out and shouts 'Oy! Are you crossing or what? Come on, love!' And then he's gone with a big roar. The world settles down again. No sign of anyone but me. I walk home.

If I left Mary's at seven how is it I don't get home until nearly half past? Has it taken half an hour to walk half a mile? It's a bit like one of those Eleven Plus sums I never got the hang of; if a car travels at thirty miles an hour and stops three times for forty minutes, and he puts three gallons in at two o clock, what does he have for his tea? I don't even try to answer it. I say 'Mary's Mammy is very nice' and Mum says 'What's that got to do with anything?' and I look at our white and gold striped wallpaper and the washing up waiting for me, and the to-do list and I don't know what I can say that will make things better, so in my head I say 'Go away, go away, please make her go in to watch the TV with Dad, and leave me alone.' And I wait for her to say 'Oh, get out of my sight' which she always does, and she does. And it's lovely to close the kitchen door and run the hot water, and start the washing up with Adam Faith drying and Nancy sitting at the little table with Gilbert Harding and Charlie Drake asking twenty questions. Gilbert says 'Is it a human animal?' And I say 'Yes' and Charlie says 'Ha...llo, my darling. Is the human a female?' And I say 'Yes' and Alma Cogan says 'Is she alive or dead?' And I say 'Alive' and she turns back into Nancy Spain. Charlie shouts 'Diana Dors' and I say no. Gilbert says 'Is she a villain?' And my eyes prickle and my throat itches and my breaths come in big lumps and I say 'No, she fucking isn't.' As I wash Mum's pyrex pie dish I look at the picture in the window, at the brightly lit reflection of the kitchen, and there's no Gilbert, no Nancy or Alma, no Charlie. There's just me. No Adam Faith drying up with his lisp. I nearly understood something today. I know that I'm very very close to understanding something important but it keeps melting away. With my bad brain.

I say out loud 'It's me.'

I go into the sitting room because it's Friday so I can stay up until eight o'clock but Daddy looks at me and I know they've been talking and he says 'We give you an inch and you take a mile. Will you never learn?' And Mum says 'Off to bed.' and as I nearly close the door Daddy says 'Straight to sleep.' So I close the door and go upstairs.

I can't go straight to sleep, no matter how hard I try. So Clint comes in and says 'Shove up a bit, honey' and I do and he lies next to me and he smells quite like Mary's Dad.

MOSS BROS

Maroon knickers. They are horrible. But everything else is smashing. We were in the shop for hours, and Mum had the list from the convent so we wouldn't forget anything; beige socks (knee), white socks (ankle, PE), maroon skirt, white blouse, the list went on and on all the way to maroon knickers. Uniform knickers! Wait till I tell Aunty Nelly.

It's so new to me, what'cha do to me

I've put one of everything – not the PE stuff – on my bed, like I'm wearing it, so there's this person who's invisible on the white candlewick spread and all we can see of her is her clothes. The socks are on the bit between the bed and the floor so it looks like she's been standing there and has just flopped back but her feet are on the floor. I'm going to call her Penny, because Mum kept saying 'This is costing a pretty penny.' Pretty Penny.

The shop was all brown wood and very quiet like a church but when you got used to it, it was OK. Nice. I had to try everything on and every time the lady said 'There – perfect!' Mum said 'Hmm... maybe the next size up, or maybe two sizes... can we try two sizes up?' And I'd have to go back in the curtained bit and take off that skirt or blouse or jumper and hand it out and the lady would put a hand through and give me one two sizes up. The lady was very nice and she started off really smiley and said things like

'Senior school! How exciting!' but after a long long time and lots of trying ons, she wasn't so smiley and when Mum said 'Is there only one size of scarf?' there was this long silence and the lady took a deep breath and didn't let it out again and the man who was on the men's counter came over really quickly and told her it was time for her break. He was nice too, and when Mum wanted to get the next size up in gaberdines he said that would be a good idea because then I could shelter the rest of the class when it rained. And possibly a couple of teachers. Even Mum laughed and I didn't have to try on the next size after all. It's still right down to my ankles, nearly.

Then as they were wrapping everything up, these two girls came in, wearing the summer uniform and they looked smashing. Their boaters were all battered with flowers stuck in the bands, and they were laughing and talking and they knew the shop lady and she knew them and they said only one more year to go. The lady introduced me and they said they'll look out for me in September. They were beautiful. The shop lady said 'You'll need new boaters next summer, girls.' and the tall one said 'No, these are coolio.' Coolio! They must be allowed to say that in the convent. I won't tell Dad. The short one handed over a piece of paper and said 'Only a few bits and bobs – I'll collect them the last week of August' and the shop lady said 'You said that last year and when did you deign to turn up? October!' But she wasn't cross and the girl said 'Ooops!' and pretended to be sorry and her friend shoved her and she nearly knocked over a display of ties. They said they had to fly because they were late again and when they charged to the door the man called out 'Oy! You two!' And they turned around and he said 'Don't do anything I wouldn't do' and they laughed and ran out and it all felt really empty and sad and I wished they would come back. That's going to be me soon. I'll be one of those tall, happy, noisy girls and the people in the shop will know me and we'll joke and me and my friend, Pretty Penny, will dash everywhere and have things to run to and we'll not have Mum with us, or anyone.

It was very quiet when they'd gone. The man looked at me and said 'That'll be you in a few year's time' and it was like he could read my mind. I was so happy. I am so happy. I can't wait, I can't wait, I can't wait. Two months and I'll be there. I'll be them.

Hot diggity,
dog ziggity boom,
what'cha do to me,
when you're holdin' me tight!

We have five hundred name tapes to sew on my uniform. Enough, Dad says, to last for the whole of my school career. They came in the post from Cash's, and some are red and some are black. My job is to thread the needle for Mum, and to take the finished ones upstairs and put them in their proper homes. She's put little notices on the dressing table drawers and on the wardrobe and even in the airing cupboard.

It's the summer holidays now so Dad's at work and Mum's stuck here, trying to be nice but her eyes don't look at me and we don't know what to do with ourselves. She goes to the Home and Colonial two days a week and I can sing and dance and talk to the air and I run up the stairs into their bedroom and I say really loud to the bed 'You're horrible, you're horrible, you're horrible.' They are good days. On the days when she's here I try not to breathe because my breathing fills the whole house and Norah can hear it however much she tries not to. She can't un-know that I'm here and that Anthony isn't, no matter how hard she tries. I don't know how I know but I do. Mary has gone over to Ireland to see her Grandma but my Grandma, who is not my Grandma really but Mrs Donaghue or Mum's Mum, lives near Brighton and we can't go there until Dad passes his driving test. Not before the age of miracles, then.

Martin sends a letter every week, on air mail paper and he has very tiny writing so he crams a lot in and then does one of his funny drawings. He drew me in convent uniform, knocking a policeman's hat off. I don't know why.

Some days Mum sends me for eggs all the way to the egg farm, which is an hour's walk but it's a lovely lane and it's a good thing to do. We need a lot of eggs and some days she sends me for six and the next day she sends me for another six. I am out from under her feet for two hours and a bit more because I dawdle and talk to the cows and when I get home Mum never tells me off for taking too long. I wish I could stay out all day. In the afternoon I do the weeding. I have a cushion and I kneel on it and have a little fork and I weed the flower beds. The garden is long but very thin and there's a boring lawn and all around it is a boring flower bed, planted with marigolds. Hundreds of the things. I hate the cat pee smell of marigolds almost as much as I hate weeding so I try not to think about it and just imagine the convent. Before they left, Mary lent me all her *Malory Towers* books, six of them, and said that this is exactly what it's going to be like, except we won't be boarding. But that's good, because it means we'll walk to the station together and catch a train every single day all the way from Chippenham to Bath. It's going to be cool. *Malory Towers* is by Enid Blyton so I can only read them in bed, but I think Mary's right – the convent is going to be exactly like that.

Mary says that I am Belinda in the books and I have to tell her who she is when she gets back. This is a problem because I think she's Sally, who is sensible and good, but I think she would like to be Alicia who is very clever and quick. Belinda is a bit bonkers so she's right about me. I think I'll say she is a little bit sensible but also clever and funny, which she almost is, so she's a new person entirely and her name is Sallicia.

I can't wait. I go to sleep every night hoping that I'll slip into a coma like they kept waiting for Mammy to do, and wake up just a day before term starts.

I still have the horse dream but it's not as bad as it was because right at the start of the dream, when I first see the horse, I know that he's grazing on my Mammy's grave so it's not a terrible shock and although I still wave my arms and can't move, stuck in treacle, and although I can't shout and instead still manage a smothered sort of fmummf, it doesn't scare me any more. Uncle Alf is another matter entirely.

When I get into bed I read until it's too dark, then I pray for Martin in the jungle and for Mammy's soul and that's getting better – at least two decades every single night which must be making inroads just in case Father Sullivan was wrong and she's still there – and then it's Clint or Violette or riding to the ridge where the west commences. And the cotton wool trees. And as I start feeling sleepy the convent pops into my head and I'm so happy and my head wanders off into Malory Towers and all the things I'll do with all my new friends and it's heaven. I'll be leaving at seven every morning and I won't be back until 5.15 at the earliest.

Never knew that my heart could go 'zing' thattaway
Ting-a-ling thattaway, make me sing thattaway

Then it's morning and I have butterflies and I work out how many days before school starts and today it's seventeen. After today, it's two more Sundays.

No breakfast because I'm going to Holy Communion so we just have a cup of tea. This is not so great because if the Mass goes on for a bit I start going woozy and I have to sit down and stick my head between my legs and a little bit of sick, which Mum says is bile and perfectly normal, comes into my mouth. Mum says I have to try to rise above it. If I get woozy I should concentrate on the Mass, pray harder and rise above. Not everything has to be about me and she'd like to get through one Mass without me clamouring for attention.

Daddy takes his driving test this week so maybe, next Sunday, we'll arrive in style. We sit by the BVM statue so that Mum can light a candle for the repose of the soul of Anthony Gerard and she kneels down there, all alone, putting one hand under each elbow, so she's made a sort of cradle with her arms, as if there was a baby in them, and I feel that sorry for her. She always does this when she lights a candle but you can see she doesn't even know she's doing it. She never held Anthony. They wouldn't let her. He lived for six whole weeks and they never let her hold him even once. Her heart is broken and no one can mend it. Sometimes you can see her broken heart.

There's a bit of a commotion behind us and I look round and Mary's back from Ireland, with her mam and her sisters, all piling into a long pew and filling it. The baby's already grizzling and Pat's pulling a face like she doesn't want to be with them, but Mary's waving like mad and I do a tiny finger wave back. Mary's gone all freckled and red and she makes the secret sign we agreed, the sign that says 'Sisters, for ever and all eternity.' And I am so happy. Again I am so happy. Even when the old priest comes in, the English one who gives sermons that last three days, I am so happy.

Said 'goodbye' to my troubles, they went thattaway
Ever since you came into my life!
Hot diggity, dog ziggity boom, what'cha do to me-

I know that everything isn't about me, and I manage fine until the Kyrie Eleison, which is the only part of the Latin Mass that's Greek, and probably my favourite, but then it all goes a bit grey and wobbly. God have mercy on us, Christ have mercy on us. You know that feeling you get, when the spit comes into your mouth and your brain moves slower than your head if you try to look up? Dad looks at me and lifts his eyebrows. I start to say something but then I hear this almighty crash, but I don't see anything any more, not until I open my eyes and my head is wedged under the pew in front and all I can see is shoes and dust and an old hot water pipe. You'd think they'd keep a holy place a bit cleaner. Then there's a bit of a tussle and I'm in the porch and Dad's shoving my head between my knees and he doesn't mean to but he's cutting off my throat and I can't breathe and my eyes are watering from all the bile that is normal. One of the old nuns from the retirement home down the road comes out with a glass of water but all I can see is her feet and I'm trying to wave my arms to tell them I can't breathe and Dad lets go of my head to take the water and I take a big gulp and sit up. 'There!' Says the old nun, 'Praise God, she's back with us,' like I'd been dying, but if I'd died it would have been strangulation and Daddy would have been charged with murder.

Mum's mortified. She tells us that,when she comes out a few minutes later. Dad says it happens and not to worry but she says we've missed the Consecration and if we don't get back in quickly we'll miss Communion and then she goes back in. We follow her after a minute or two and Dad says 'You can skip Communion today' but I shake my head. I join the end of the Communion line and when I pass Mary she pretends to swoon and lies there on her pew like she's dead and I try not to laugh but she's funny, is Mary. Maybe she's a bit Belinda too.

I've settled myself by the time I kneel down at the altar rail, and I take the blessed body of Christ into my mouth and I try not to touch him with my teeth and I say sorry for the bile, and he says it's OK, I couldn't help it. And before I swallow him, which is completely and utterly the best part of life, that moment when Christ is in you and you feel so holy you could bloody well fly, I sing to him, a little tiny silent song, to show him how great it is that I'm off to La Sainte Union Convent and to say thank you that he's making me one of the beautiful strong girls in a straw hat with flowers and a laugh like a bell. What I sing to him isn't a hymn but I sing it anyway because I'm so happy

Never knew that my heart could go 'zing' thattaway
Ting-a-ling thattaway, make me sing thattaway
Said 'goodbye' to my troubles, they went thattaway,
hot diggity, dog ziggity, boom what you do to me
How my future will shine
Hot diggity, dog ziggity, boom what you do to me
How my future will shine.

THREE LITTLE MAIDS
FROM SCHOOL ARE WE

Dad sang that as we drove to the station for my first day at the convent. Yes, drove. The age of miracles is upon us. He passed his test, not the first time he took it, but the second, which is good, even if he did drive straight into the gate post on his way home. Then he backed into the neighbour's wall but the wall's OK and no one saw. The car's only a little bit dented. So we drove to the station this morning and he sang 'Three Little Maids' to me and it was a very happy drive. We didn't hit anything at all and the crunchy noise when he does the gears isn't as bad as it used to be and people don't turn to look when they hear us coming any more. Well, not always. And when he kangaroo hops we cheer. If Mum's in the car we don't.

The train's leaving the station and Dad's on the platform, and Mary's mam, and a few others all waving. We'll be back at five but we all wave back and it's like we're going off to the Army, only then it was Dad on the train and me and Mammy on the platform. But that's not true because he always went in an army lorry from the barracks and we never waved him off because he hates goodbyes. I just make things up all the time.

Mary takes her hat off as soon as we're out of sight so I do too and then everyone else does. There's five new girls from Chippenham. We don't know the other three. We just look at each other for a bit and then we hear a shout from down the carriage and there's a huge gang of convent girls and they're all kissing and hugging and telling each other what they did in the holidays and the grown ups smile at each other and one man says to another man 'There goes our peace and quiet' and the other man says 'Roll on half-term' and I say 'Give us a chance, we've not even started yet' and the men look surprised and Mary says 'Here she goes' and everyone laughs and suddenly it's OK. Maybe if I could talk like that at home, to Dad and Mum, they'd start to like me.

Pert as a school-girl well can be
Filled to the brim with girlish glee

I can't believe I'm here, sitting on a train without a single grown up to ruin everything. In my new uniform only two sizes too big. If Aunty Nelly could see me now! Or Mammy. Don't think about Mammy.

One of the other new girls, called Jennifer, asks what my accent is and I say I'm an Army brat so it's a big mix of stuff and they look impressed. They sound a bit like Mum who comes from Croydon and a bit like Mary who is Chippenham born and bred. Jennifer's uniform is two sizes too big too. We can't stop talking. One of them has a pony and one of them has a dog but one of them doesn't have anything so I'm not the only one. Jennifer's Dad is a bus conductor and Lynda's is a solicitor. We agree that we'll be friends all through school and will become known as the Gang.

We get off at Bath Spa where there's a Sixth Former waiting to walk to the convent with us but she's not friendly and she keeps saying that we have to remember the way because she won't be walking us back tonight. It's dead simple. Straight down, and right at the Parade. I tell her this and she says 'Don't come crying to me if you get lost' and I say that would be difficult, if I was lost.

Unless she was lost too. She says I won't last long with that attitude, but I wasn't being rude, I was just saying. Mary gets the giggles and this Sixth Former, who didn't even tell us her name, says it's rude to laugh. It isn't. But I don't say anything else because the butterflies have started up and I can see that it's the same for Mary. The convent is getting nearer, huge and grey, and we all stop talking. This is it. This is it.

Our coats go in a cloakroom in something called the basilica because it's nearly under the ground, in something called the Tin Hut, because it's a tin hut. And then we have to go up three stairs, down a corridor, turn left in to a big long corridor, turn left into a big wide staircase and this is the New Building. It's very smart. The hall is up the stairs and it's huge and empty with a shiny floor. Not quite empty, there are a few girls sitting at the front and the horrible sixth former tells us to get a chair and wait. So we do. She goes and I feel sick with excitement. I look at Mary but she's staring at the floor and looks like I feel in the Mass. If she faints there's no pew to catch her, she'll hit the floor at thirty miles an hour and never be the same again.

A nun comes in and she's quite old and sweet and she says it's a grand day for everyone and the start of a big adventure and the butterflies get worse. I put my hand up and ask if I can go to the toilet and then someone else does and someone else. The nun points out a door just outside the hall and we all head off towards it, and Mary grabs my hand, and others join us and by the time we get there it's a whole crowd of us, and the nice old nun calls out 'Quickly, girls, quickly!'. There's a long row of toilets with blue shiny doors and the place is sparkling. I thought I was going to be sick, but I'm not. I just do the smallest wee the world has ever known and when I come out Mary has gone but a blond girl is waiting to go in and she's the last. She grabs my arm and says

'Wait for me?' because she doesn't want to walk back into that huge hall all on her own with everyone looking so I say yes. While I wait I look at myself in the mirror. I don't look like me any more. I wonder if Cheyenne would help at all, or Perry, but before I can decide, the girl, who says her name is Beth, comes out and we walk back to the hall together.

When the head mistress comes in everything goes very still. There are three teachers with her, all of them civilians, not nuns, and they're all normal but she's very small and very fat and her name is Madam Bernard Xavier and she's quite pink and jolly but her eyes are like brown glass, teddy bear eyes, that look right into you and know everything. I think I would like her to be my friend – I think she would be very sharp and funny, like Nancy Spain but holier. You have to call all the nuns Madam, because the order of nuns was started in France a thousand years ago. Not a thousand. Less. Their wimples aren't proper wimples like the nuns in Omagh, they're just like the paper you get inside a packet of biscuits. Corrugated. Maybe that's what they do, just buy loads of biscuits. She looks at us all and she laughs, and the old nun laughs too and the teachers smile and the head mistress says 'You look terrified, girls. We don't bite. We may have the occasional nibble but I promise we won't bite' and we laugh too and it all goes a bit phew. It wasn't a great joke. But it was a valiant attempt. Like Captain Horatio Hornblower's attack to leeward. Concentrate, concentrate, listen to what she's saying. It's all about great opportunity and loyalty and if we're devoted to them they'll be devoted to us. Or committed. Something anyway. I'm busy looking at everyone's satchels and wondering why I've got a case. I liked my case till I saw their satchels.

We've all had letters telling us which form we're in, Madam says, and do we all remember? There's silence. No one dares say a word. She asks again. A few of us nod (I don't) and then she gives up and says that all the girls who are in 1X go to the right with Mrs Rawle, and a tall gingery teacher goes to where she's pointing. 'All the girls in 1Y step over there with Miss Bray' and another small crowd follow a smart little lady in a baby pink skirt suit. And all the girls in 1W can stay exactly where they are with Miss Cooper. So, we get the blushing, lip chewing one with fat ankles, thick glasses and buck teeth. I like her. There are a few more words from the head mistress and I don't hear any of them, then we all file out behind our teachers. 1X goes first and Jenny waves to me as she passes, and then 1Y goes out and Mary, who looks OK again, mutters 'Help! I'm being kidnapped.' as she passes us. We follow Miss Cooper to our form room. It's in the Tin Hut and it's got a big high ceiling and big high windows you can't see out of unless you stand on a chair, and old desks and a lovely smell of chalk and education.

Miss Cooper tells us we're her very first form. She finished her training last year and she teaches Latin and RE. She smiles too much and she's frightened of us.

Everything is a source of fun
Nobody's safe, for we care for none

Beth is in 1W too and we end up sitting next to each other. Miss Cooper says we can talk quietly while she looks for the register and sorts out her desk. Beth tells me straight away, like it matters a lot, that she's a twin but her sister passed the Eleven Plus and went to Bath High School. Beth came here because she failed and she's happy about that because she wanted to come here anyway. I say I spectacularly failed half of the exam, which is what Mum told Father Sullivan, and just scraped through half of it, which isn't true but I don't want to make Beth feel bad. She says that 1W is for girls who failed, and 1Y is for girls who passed but aren't madly clever, and 1X is for girls who are amazingly genius. We both pull the same face at the idea of being an amazing genius and then we laugh. I don't know why, but we can't stop laughing. We just laugh and laugh and even Miss Cooper smiles before she gets a bit cross and then says let's not start off on the wrong foot and that it isn't at all funny but we think it is, because that's how we are today, and we nearly wet ourselves. The girl sitting behind us, who says her name is Lisa, puts her hand up and says that there's dried up snot stuck under her desk and that does it. We all go 'Eugh!' And a girl from South Africa shouts 'Siss!' And someone else says she's going to be sick. Everyone's on their hands and knees looking under the desks for more snot. The great snot hunt. The room is in happy uproar and Miss Cooper is wringing her hands and shouting 'Girls! Girls! Settle down now' and her voice is all panickey. I say not to worry, it'll be Catholic snot and Beth says she's Protestant and it's just the funniest thing ever. A girl with glasses says we should pray to the patron saint of snot and Miss Cooper flaps her hands at us and tears come to her eyes and I wish I could stop laughing but I can't. I just can't.

Life is a joke that's just begun
Three little maids from school

The door slams open and the laughing stops. Bang! A small woman is there, a nun, and she has a square chin and thin lips and steel rimmed glasses and she stands there, saying absolutely nothing. It's like the wireless has been turned off. We all stop laughing, like magic. The silence is terrible. Lisa, who is a big girl and started the whole snot thing is stuck under her desk with her bum sticking out. She can't see what's going on and she says, all cross and bothered, 'I'm flipping wedged – give us a hand, someone.' And the nun steps forward and bends down and takes her elbow and helps her up. When she comes eyeball to eyeball with the glinting glasses, Lisa sort of yelps. It's awful. Miss Cooper takes a step towards her and then stops. It's awful. It's so awful.

When it starts all over again, it's my fault. I start to laugh and Beth starts to laugh and then it spreads like a blush and we're helpless. The nun glares at Miss Cooper and sort of hisses 'You have two minutes.' And then she's gone. But the great thing is, Miss Cooper has started laughing as well, and she puts her finger to her lips, sort of begging us, and we shush each other and bite our lips and cover our mouths and bit by bit the room grows quieter. There are still snorts and gasps and a few sighs and people blowing their noses and coughing but it's mostly quiet. Miss Cooper smiles at us all and says 'Thank you, girls' and everything's OK. She takes the register and we open our desks and put our new pencil cases in them.

Everything is a source of fun
Nobody's safe, for we care for none
Life is a joke that's just begun
Three little maids from school.

MAKING SPORT

We've got our timetables and we've been given our own peg and shoe box in the new cloakroom in the new building, and the basilica is only to be used for changing for PE and there are lots of other things we have to remember, like where the milk is at playtime, next to the gym in a little yard by the old building which is where all the old nuns go to die. And where the chapel is, and the Mother Superior's office. After milk there's bells ringing everywhere and we have to go back to the classroom and everyone's useless – half of them come in late because they were lost but you can't get lost, can you, if you're looking for a bloody big tin building and it has just one corridor and your room has 1W on the door? Beth and me are the first back and I think we're going to be really good friends. Her Dad works in the big Admiralty building near the Parade and she's travelled around a bit too, not as much as me but a fair bit.

It's Tuesday and we look at our timetables to see what happens next and it says 'Elocution' and Beth says 'Get wired up and have your brains boiled' and we get the giggles. We're the only ones who know what elocution is so I tell them, it's speaking, and they are all impressed. I don't know how I know that but I do. Oh, yes, I remember. Mum said elocution will sort out my thees and tha's.

Miss Holland, who is about eighty and has brown teeth, comes in and says she's going to teach us how to sound like ladies and she writes something on the board and it says 'There's a big red dragon and he's running though the town.' And we repeat it after her and she says oh no, that won't do at all. We have to say it, over and over, taking big breaths and rolling the 'r's and pulling faces, opening our eyes as far as they'll go, and I turn and look at Lisa and all the others and they all look demented. We're going 'Therrrre's a big rrrred drrrragon and he's rrrrrunning though the town.' and everyone's trying not to laugh. Miss Holland says that's lovely. She gives us a piece of paper each and it's a poem and tells us to practice it in pairs, so I read it to Beth and she reads it to me. Then the bell goes and Miss Holland says that our homework is to learn the poem and to recite it at our next lesson, on Thursday.

Bring Samson in, cried someone in the crowd,
And one fat priest of Dagon cried aloud 'Oh, excellent!
Excellent sport to see a blind man baited'

The day is full and the dinner is lovely, brown meat and potatoes and lovely gravy and yellow cake and bright yellow custard. We eat in the new hall and there's a hatch they open and you see the kitchen and women in white overalls. I'm in the queue with Beth and there's an older girl behind us and she groans and says 'Oh, no, Fishface' and it turns out the nice nun from this morning is called Fishface because she has a face like a fish. And she does, a bit. The girl groaned because Fishface teaches French and the girl did really badly in last terms exam. I say 'Bad luck' and she says no, not really, they all did really badly because Fishface is a disaster. I'm not sure what she means so I just get my custard and cake. Fishface comes over and says to the girl 'Well, then, Elaine, we are going to do better this term, aren't we?' And Elaine says 'Yes, Madam.' But as Fishface walks away all the girls make these gruesome faces and they're laughing.

'Fishface, Fishface, to make sport! A happy thought.' Which is sad.

Beth and me practice the Samson poem in playtime. We do all the open eyes, big mouth, starey bits and get the laughs again. If I stay till upper sixth, which I hope I do, I'll have seven whole years of this. I suddenly panic and grab Beth's arm 'your Dad won't get posted away, will he?' And she says probably not. He's just a pen pusher now and I say 'Snap! So is my Dad.' And we laugh.

And suddenly the walls regurgitated

The second morning I wake up and realise straight away that today is good. And I didn't have the horse dream last night either. Or Uncle Alf. I walk to the station and meet Mary waiting outside her house. We came home on the train together last night and I said the Samson poem to her and she showed me her first Latin lesson, which we will have on Thursday. She said Miss Cooper is a terrible nervous teacher and I said she's my form teacher and she's nice. Mary's form teacher is the small one in pink and she said she's very strict, which is odd because she looks like Kathy Kirby who isn't at all strict. I told her that regurgitate means being sick or burping and she said they must have had weird walls then, and I said the real word's reverberated but we've taken artistic licence. She didn't get the joke. Beth got it straight away.

Coming home was different yesterday. Mum was at the door, waiting for me, and she asked me how it went. I said it was smashing and she seemed to wait for me to say some more so I said the nuns were very nice and she asked if we'd been to Chapel. She was disappointed we'd just said a prayer at assembly and the Angelus at 12, but then she tapped the to-do list and said that now I was growing up there were a few changes, I could clean her shoes and Daddy's too, when I did mine. When I went into the shed there were two pairs next to the shoe cleaning box, Dad's good brown ones and her black ones.

I'd not had time for Clint or Cliff or Val Doonican or anyone all day so I caught up with them as I cleaned the shoes and when they were there it was a bit like coming home. I like the shed, it smells a little bit dusty and old-grassy and cleaning shoes is a good thing to do. I'm a real soldier's daughter when it comes to shoes.

When I was still eating my boiled egg Dad came home because the train and everything means I get back only a few minutes before him. He called out to Mum but he didn't go into the kitchen! Instead he came and sat down opposite me, where his place was laid, and he said 'Come on then, Convent Miss, tell me everything.' and I did and it was gorgeous. He smiled all the time and when I told him about elocution he was impressed and said I'd soon be reading the news on the TV at this rate. Mum came in with his cottage pie and pretended to be surprised that he was there. 'I didn't hear you come in!' But she did. If she hadn't heard him, why would she bring in his cottage pie? I am going to concentrate my brain and work out why things happen.

I fell asleep trying to work out how many days were left at the convent before I'm seventeen but with my brain and not knowing about holidays, and having to multiply everything by seven which is impossible, it was all a bit messy and I gave up.

Every day, when we get off the train, we see other girls all heading the same way, some from the station and some from other roads and they look just like us and we look just like them, but in longer coats. It's like I'm up in a cloud, looking down, and seeing all the little maroon and yellow blobs heading towards the big grey convent, like little ants. And I am one of them. I am so happy, I could die with happiness.

Lars Porsena of Clusium

I've not even been here two weeks and I'm in trouble with three of the teachers. Not big 'tell your father' trouble but I'm getting a name for myself. That's what Fishface said. Whose real name is Madam Mary Agnes.

Just like Mary Lord, Miss Holland didn't get the joke when the whole class chanted 'And suddenly the walls regurgitated'. Then I asked who Dagon was and she looked blank so I said 'The one with the fat priest' and she frowned at me and said did it matter and when I shrugged she went potty. Shrugging is not allowed in elocution and when Beth accidentally called it Electrocution Miss Holland went all stiff and her head went wobbly. We both have to learn at least eight lines of a poem for punishment but we like learning poems so that's OK. We had to choose one from a little green book so we've gone for 'Horatius' because it isn't cissy and I'm the daughter of a soldier and Beth's the daughter of a sailor. Sort of. And it's fab. We go into the corner of the netball court at playtime and we act it out.

By the Nine Gods he swore
That the great house of Tarquin
Should suffer wrong no more.

I'm just getting used to being in trouble with La Holland (as Lisa calls her) when blow me, this prefect who is also called Lisa tells me to stop running in the corridor and I wasn't, I was speed walking like Dr Barbra Moore who walked from John o' Groats to Land's End without even spending a penny on the way. And this Lisa, who shall henceforth be known as Mona Lisa to make it clear which one we're on about, said I was being cheeky. So I had to go

and knock on the door of the staff room which is in another building called Saint Anne's and tell the duty teacher what happened.
And the duty teacher, wouldn't you know it, is only Old Square
Chin, the nun who came in and gave Miss Cooper two minutes on
our first day. She says 'Yes?' And I say 'I was sent here because a
prefect said I was running, which is a lie because one heel was on
the floor at all times, like Dr Barbara Moore, and that is definitely
not running.' And this nun stared at me and opened her mouth but
no words came out and then she just shut the door in my face! In
my face! Didn't say anything at all. So I walked back down the
corridor and past Mona Lisa and she said I'd obviously not been
to the staff room and she gave me a bad mark! A bad mark! For
not running in the corridor and having a door shut in my face.

Three bad marks and you get a detention which is two hours
on a Saturday and Mum will have kittens. Not nice cuddly little
kittens either, kittens with great big claws and blood stained teeth.

By the Nine Gods he swore it,
And named a trysting day,

And then we had a Latin lesson and Miss Cooper was very
nervous and we were all quite fidgetty and it was very boring and
all about what you call a farmer in Latin, which seems to be about
fifteen different words. Miss Cooper said that we had better start
concentrating because 'Tempus Fewgit' so I said 'Fugit' with a
hard 'g' and short vowels and she said 'What did you say?' all
cold and not at all frightened of me. I said it again 'Fugit' and she
told me to stand in the corridor until the end of lesson when she
would deal with me. I said 'My Dad says that' and she said 'I don't
care what obscenities your father comes out with, Lucy Gannon,
you do not use that language here.' When I was standing in the

corridor, which is very boring and not very nice because the Tin
Hut is an old and dusty building and you feel very lonely, Old
Square Chin came along and I knew for certain I was going to be
in Big Trouble. She stopped and asked me what I'd been doing
NOW? And when I told her and said 'But she's not the only one –
the whole church gets it wrong from the Pope down' she said 'Your
father's a classicist, is he?' And I said 'No, he's a County Court
Clerk' and she shook her head at me but smiley and I couldn't make
her out at all. She went into the classroom but just then the bell
went and when she came back out again she was with Miss Cooper
and they were both smiling and Miss Cooper said 'Back in you go.'
and squeezed my arm like we were friends or something.

I am trying very hard to concentrate but some things are just too
impossible. Anyway, old steel glasses is called Madam
Evangelista but her nickname is 'Der Feuhrer' and she teaches Latin
and Greek and she is a big cheese. If she was in the Army she'd be
scrambled eggs. Beth and me know what that means. It's like having
a secret language. A code. We could be in the French Resistance
together. If it was still the war, and if we were French. And a bit older.

Me and Beth practised our poem when we were changing for
gym and I jumped up on the lockers and she climbed onto a sink
and we declaimed, like Miss Holland said, and we did the whole
poem, well, not quite, but a lot of it. Everyone stood around, getting changed, into those horrible big gym knickers, and we did all
the verses we knew, which was two.

Lars Porsena of Clusium By the Nine Gods he swore

Miss Holland said it's all about speaking from underneath your
rib cage and throwing the words into the air like slingshots, so we
took great big breaths and slung them out.

That the great house of Tarquin
Should suffer wrong no more.
By the Nine Gods he swore it,
And named a trysting day,
And bade his messengers ride forth,
East and west and south and north,
To summon his array.

When we did the east and west bit we both pointed but accidentally I went left and Beth went right and it was funny and Lisa
cheered. And then we started sort of shouting it, because it was so
exciting, and you could see everyone was enjoying it and this time,
when we pointed, everyone else did too, and it was like we were
in one of Father Sullivan's grand filums.

East and west and south and north
The messengers ride fast,
And tower and town and cottage
Have heard the trumpet's blast.

Gillian Walters was trying to join in but she didn't even know the
poem and she'd got one leg in the knickers and she was wobbling
around on the other, and Lisa told her to shut up because she was
ruining it.

Shame on the false Etruscan
Who lingers in his home,
When Porsena of Clusium
Is on the march for Rome.

When we got to 'Rome' it was really loud and we pointed at the ceiling like it was the way we were going, onwards and upwards, and we were breathless and everyone was impressed. Someone clapped but it wasn't one of us, it was in the doorway and it was Mrs Ash, our English teacher who is very nice but quite strict, and she said 'We could hear you upstairs, girls.' and we jumped down and said sorry, and she said 'No, it was very stirring. Well done.' And walked away.

I don't get it.

THE PARTY

I may have been wrong about Mrs Ash. She is very friendly and seems like she's nice but we just got our first English essays back and I have to stop saying '*and*', '*lovely*' and '*nice*'. I also have to say '*which is*' a bit less, which is impossible. And I should try to find another way of saying '*a bit*' and '*stuff*'. I had the highest mark of all the essays but it was still only 6 out of 10, which is a bit mean. And we shouldn't say '*we walked round*' unless we are spherical. Which we are not. We should say '*we walked around.*' But then she read my essay out and we all enjoyed it, even me, because it's like someone else wrote it because she read it like it was proper English, not Golborne. She said she looked forward to teaching me for the next seven years, which was lovely. Nice. It's not going to be easy.

I have to go through my essay and underline all the words she talked about and there are thirty two *and*s, seven *nice*s and four *lovely*s. Which doesn't seem that terrible. And I wrote *which* five times, and there were two *stuff*s but only one *bit* so I don't know what all the fuss was about. My full stops are too haphazard and I mustn't shove one down and then have second thoughts and bung in another two words. Like this. I thought I was going to be good at English but now I'm not good at anything much. It's OK though, because no one else is, either.

For homework we have to write two sides about The Party. I've never been to a party. That's not true, I have, but it was years ago and it was very boring. I went to a wedding party in Cyprus with that old EOKA man and two women who spat at me, but that's too rude to put in a proper essay. I'm a bit stuck. Mrs Ash said it's good to have a flight of fancy but try to make it real. She reads us poetry but it's good, not stupid 'Dragons Rushing Through the Town', and then she said that because Beth and me were so good at reciting it, we could all study 'Horatius' and it's even better than we thought it was.

> *To every man upon this earth*
> *Death cometh soon or late.*

Which is true, when you think about it, and it gave me an idea about my essay.

The Party That Never Was Lucy Gannon 1W
When I was nearly seven and we lived in Ulster my Mammy said I could have a birthday party because I'd never had one, except for Egypt which didn't count because I got heat stroke and ended up in bed with a mosquito net and a metal bowl to be sick in. We were a right pair that day, me in my room being sick and moaning and Mammy in hers with the thing in her head, which we didn't know about yet. It was a good party, even without the birthday girl to blow out the candles. That's what my friend Barry told me the next day, when he came to see if I was still alive. Which I was.

But now we were in Ulster so there was no danger of me getting heat stroke this time. Mammy said I could have a cake and we were going to play musical chairs and pass-the-parcel. My Aunty Nelly came all the way from

Lancashire to Omagh to help, because Mammy saw two dustbin men when there was only one and she said 'How funny! They must be twins.' And Daddy went very quiet and I knew it was something important but didn't know what. After that sometimes Mammy couldn't see and it was all a nuisance and she would laugh when she dropped things but I didn't think it was funny because you'd pick it up, the book or the spoon and put it back in her hand and she'd drop it all over again. Sometimes when she laughed I thought maybe she was crying, but she wasn't. She told me. Aunty Nelly came to make the tea so we wouldn't end up with chopped finger sandwiches instead of chopped ham.

When we'd set the table and I'd sung to Aunty Nelly about her wooden belly, just before any of the party children came, the doctor knocked on the door and took Dad into the kitchen and Aunty Nelly gave me a chocolate biscuit and told me to sit quietly and wait for everyone. The doctor's a Protestant and an Army doctor so he's not great with wives, that's what Dad says, trench foot and shrapnel is what he's good at. When I saw Colum, a fat lad with glasses from school, come up the path I jumped up and opened the door and he had a present for me and I was happy. Then Aunty Nelly came and said sorry but it was cancelled, and Dad went up the stairs with the doctor and his face was all grey and strange and I started crying. I wasn't crying about the party. I didn't know what I was crying about but it was something terrible, and I could feel it. I didn't like that Doctor. He was always saying 'It's probably nothing.' but you knew he just wanted to get away. Dad said he was an eedjit. Which is Irish for idiot. I never did have a birthday party. When I was eight we were living with Aunty Nelly so

Mammy could die where she grew up, and Daddy was on compassionate leave and we all had other things to think about, but I got a catapult which is what I had really prayed for. Joe Grimshaw was my new best friend and he had one so now we could have competitions. When I was nine Dad married Mum and we moved to Warminster and I didn't know anyone to invite except Louise who was a Jehovah person and didn't believe in birthdays. When I was ten, my brother Anthony had just died and Mum was very poorly with her insides. When I was eleven Mum was very sad and Dad said there was a season for everything, which meant not doing anything and being quiet. When I think of my seventh birthday party, the one that nearly happened, I can see the table and the cake and the jelly that wobbled like a belly, and I remember what it felt like when Mammy was upstairs in bed, and Aunty Nelly was crying, and how Dad closed the door after the doctor and sort of grabbed me and held me like I was a baby, but too tight. I can remember all of that really well and bright like it was just this morning, but I can't remember what happened to all that food, and the cake and everything. I don't know what happened to the wrap-the-parcel parcel. Maybe the whole party is up there in heaven with Mammy. Maybe Mammy is feeding little Anthony Gerard shimmering lumps of shining strawberry jelly on a golden spoon and his little face is laughing, and all the angels are singing 'Happy Birthday To You.' And they're awash with Carnation Milk.

The End.

It's four sides, so I should get an extra mark for that. Beth said it isn't about a party, it's about me and my Mammy and I said no, it's about jelly and the cake and all that and where it went to. And I'm not bloody doing it again. It's a stupid thing to have to write about anyway. I hope we get something better next week. Something brave and fearless and noble and heroic. Three 'ands'. I don't care. That essay has put me in a right mood. Beth never swears even though she's a Prottie. Her Mum is a Brown Owl and they go camping and they all have bicycles, like the Famous Five.

And how can man die better
Than facing fearful odds,
For the Ashes of his fathers,
And the temples of his gods?

There's two *'and'*s in that one little bit, so stick that in your pipe and smoke it, Mrs Ash. Her husband smokes a pipe. He comes and waits for her after school sometimes and he has one leg shorter than the other with Polio but he looks like a film star. It's very romantic.

Mrs Ash gave out the essays. I got eight out of ten this time and two red ticks and she said it was very good but there were exactly fifty *'and'*s. I imagine her, sitting in a slice of golden light from a table lamp, marking our essays, and counting, always counting.

On Saturday I dawdled over my homework, sitting at my desk in the dining room and I could tell it was annoying Mum because she kept poking her head round – *around* – the door and saying 'Still doing that homework?' and I knew she wanted me to be out in the garden weeding because me being inside aggravates her. When I'm in the house, whatever she's doing, she sort of knows that I'm there, breathing her air and filling up her house and she can't stop thinking about it and wishing I wasn't and that Anthony was there instead. I don't know how I know what she thinks but I do.

I'm going to do this every Saturday from now on, sit here with my books open and my Conway Stewart fountain pen from Aunty Nelly, so it looks like I'm working but in my head I'm riding my cayuse (and it's cottonwood trees, not cotton wool) or riding the range with Sugarfoot, or I'm the cabin girl on Nelson's flagship, because there was a lady Pope once but no one talks about that, or I'm Cheyenne's little girl and we're making grits on a camp fire. I think that's American for baked beans. Last week Dad had to drive Mum to see her parents in Brighton and they got back late so I spent a whole evening with Mary and it was lovely. We watched *Dr Kildare* and now I'm sometimes a nurse, in America, with white shoes. Dad asked what we'd done and when I told him he said 'Doctors and lawyers. That's all you watch.' Which isn't true because *Perry Mason* isn't on any more and when it comes back I probably won't be allowed. Dad said a Russian once said that the only difference between doctors and lawyers is that lawyers merely rob you but doctors rob you and then they kill you too.

I wonder if that eedjit Army doctor killed Mammy. I wouldn't be surprised.

THEY LISTENED TO
HIS HEART

La Sainte Union Convent isn't like Malory Towers. It's better. When I wake up on the first day of half-term I feel sick with disappointment. I sit at my little table, henceforth to be referred to as my desk and I write my essay and then, because the weeding is waiting and taunting me, I write another essay, and another. After a few hours Mum comes in, all prickly and aggravated and she says in that Ward Sister voice 'Out in the sunshine, please!' And I imagine a great long ward, rows and rows of beds, and a hundred weak TB sufferers shuffling out of their sheets, staggering out into yet another cloudy day with Mum in a big billowy Ward Sister's cap with wings, shooing them all. I follow them. Dr Kildare comes with us. Most people with TB write poetry. Well, not most. Some.

I've read all about TB because when we go to school on the train every morning one of the Sixth Formers, I think she's called Katherine, gets up and opens the window and one of her friends opens the window at the end of the carriage. Katherine, who is in the front, has a rolled up sheet and she holds it out of the window and sort of lets go of one end. It blows back in the speed of the train and her friend tries to grab it at her window. Sometimes she does but sometimes she can't quite manage it and it's whipped up into the air like a plume of brilliant white smoke, but Katherine always has one end so it never blows away. It's a banner and it says 'Hello Mum!' They do this just before we come out of a tunnel because up on the hill, when the daylight crashes in again, there's Winsley TB hospital, and Katherine's Mum is in there. So she looks out every morning and sees this and knows that her daughter is thinking of her and she waves a white towel and Katherine knows that her Mum is thinking of her too. And it's lovely. And when Katherine pulls the banner in, she's all laughy and her hair is all over the place and everyone smiles. And it's also sad which is funny. Peculiar not hahah.

When it's a school day there's so much in the world to watch and listen to and think about and when it's not there's this big desert. Or moor. Or steppe. Mrs Ash says it's a fine line between being descriptive and sounding like a Thesaurus. And you don't give things capital letters just because you like them, because it's giving her a headache. She makes even a telling-off a funny and friendly thing and she says that reading my essays is like being peppered with buck shot, which is what you kill deer with so I don't think she's got that right.

I can't remember half terms when we were in the Army. I think it's because we were always in the married quarters so even when there was no school there were all your friends to play with. We've lived here for more than a year. We'd be moving soon, if Dad was still in the Army, but instead we're 'putting down roots'.

In History, which is Miss Cooper's second subject after Latin, she told us about the Roman Roads and Mary Woods said she only went on about them because the Romans spoke Latin, which I thought was a very good point. Miss Cooper is Latin mad. Roman Roads were long and straight like the ones across Salisbury Plain. Sheldon Road is long and straight and I think it may be a Roman Road. You can see the back of Sheldon Road, and the pub, from our garden, so I told Mary that our house is built on an old Roman Cemetery and at night, sometimes, if you listen very carefully, you can hear the tramp tramp tramp of marching men, and the clank of their armoured vest things. I said if it's full moon you can see a sliver of silver light on their armour. She got tears in her eyes and I thought she was crying but she swallowed hard and said no, her eyes water when she's frightened. I did that. I frightened her with my Roman Legions. I was really surprised and happy but then I felt bad so I made her laugh and it was OK.

As I do my weeding, putting stones in one apple box and dandelions in another, I think about the Romans. I can see the dust rising as they marched through Chippenhamium, and hear the feral dogs barking and the children crying as their mothers drag them indoors away from the rough men. Sometimes the Centurion looks just like Clint Walker and he slows down as he gets to me, and his soldiers march on. He looks good in the Roman stuff, a bit dusty, but still nice. Actually, Clint Walker does look sort of Italian. He never needs to say anything, he just holds out his hand. I leave my wheat threshing and follow him. He puts his arm around my shoulders and I know I am his daughter and he is my Daddy. But that's where that story ends because there's not much you can do with a marching army, apart from march. If you think about something a lot you can forget you made it up and I only went and told Miss Cooper about Sheldon Road being a troop road and Orchard Crescent being a Roman Cemetery and she looked surprised and said she'd have to look it up, and thank you for being so interested Lucy, and for contributing. And then I remembered I'd made it up but it was too late because everyone was listening. Bum. It keeps happening, that does.

I told Ellen Waterhouse that I was related to Winston Churchill but actually I think that may turn out to be true because when my Dad isn't looking like Harry Secombe, which is when he wears his new jacket for Mass, then he looks quite like Churchill. And he does a very good 'We will fight' speech. She asked if I had ever been to Number 10 Downing Street and I said no, but when he comes to Wiltshire he always stays with us, in the spare room. And that's also a possibility because it's all ready for guests but we've never had one, so if he turns up out of the blue his bed is all made up. I'm not stupid, I know it's a long shot, but Dad was in the Army for twenty-six years and he has medals and was the Army Chess Champion so it's possible. Just. Beth says I'm bonkers.

I told Anthea, who is very very good at Art, that I met Piccasso when we were in Cyprus and she believed me, Cyprus being very near Spain. She asked what he was like and I said he always had a bruise on the side of his face and she didn't understand so I said it's because he had two eyes on one side of his nose and none at all on the other side so he keeps walking into things and she hit me. We laughed and laughed. We laugh so much. Sometimes a bit of wee comes out and we tell each other and that makes us laugh even more.

We go to this little yard between the gym and the convent at morning play, and there are crates of milk and on a cold day it's delicious and on a warm day it's revolting. Geraldine Battersby, who thinks she's it, had just taken a big suck on her straw when Beth did her imitation of Madam Celine shouting 'Girls, you are so bold!'. Gerry started to laugh but she had her mouth full of milk and she was breathing in, so it all went wrong and she choked and this fountain of milk came out of her nose, and she didn't have the sense to take her mouth off the straw so we all stood there, amazed and dumbstruck like in the Bible, while the whole entire bottle, the whole entire bottle which is a third of a pint, emptied itself and her eyes were popping out and she was like this appalled frozen statue thing, amazed and stupefied, and these two streams, one from each nostril, hit the ground, splattering. It was even funnier when we did Science and Miss Rawlings drew this siphon thing on the board and it looked just like a bottle of milk and Gerry's nose.

On the second day of half-term it was Mum's birthday and we had tea. It was the first time we'd had tea for ages, since I came from Aunty Nelly. On a Saturday and Sunday I have dinner with Mum and Dad but that's all about teaching me how to eat in company, which I don't know about very much. Dad was making me laugh and there are lots of things I can't tell them about, so I was trying to think of something I could say. Because Mum says I'm sullen and I have no social graces and why don't I ever talk? Because I have dinner with them only at weekends it makes it all a bit special so I either talk too much, sort of excited, or not enough, sort of shy. I can't tell them how in Latin we take it in turns to hide in the stationary cupboard and Miss Cooper never finds out. Or how when it was raining and there were loads of umbrellas drying at the back of the class, Beth and me hid under them in Fishface's lesson. So I told them about Gillian and the milk and Dad laughed. Mum smiled. When I went into the kitchen to bring in the cakes Dad brought back from Malmesbury where he works, I heard Dad say 'For God's sake, Norah, she's a child, she can't mourn for ever.' And Mum said 'I didn't say anything, did I? I'm doing my best.' And when I came back in Dad gave me a big smile and said 'When we've had this Mum and me are going to Anthony's grave. You can watch *Blue Peter*.' So I said 'OK' and didn't tell them that *Blue Peter* isn't on on Friday. It's *Crackerjack* which Daddy doesn't like but I love. And I had a whole hour all to myself, no weeding, no homework, no Mum, just me and *Crackerjack* with Eamonn Andrews and Peter Glaze who makes me laugh. My lucky day.

I like the bit where they play Double or Drop and three children stand on little platforms and have to answer questions and for every right answer they get a silly sort of prize and for every wrong answer they get a cabbage and they end up under these great towers of things like giant rubber spiders and toilet paper and then the cabbages are piled on to the top so they can't even see and everything's wobbling. Just as this boy's stuff started to slip like an avalanche and his second cabbage hit the floor, with Peter Glaze making everything more difficult although he was trying to help, and everyone was laughing, I laughed aloud too and then I remembered how her lips go thin when I do that, but then I remembered that she was out and then I remembered how sad she is, and then I saw them in my head. My mind's eye. I saw Anthony in his little white coffin, deep in the grave, and Mum kneeling above him, weeding and weeping, and Dad standing with his pipe, watching. And I hated me for laughing. I *hated* me for laughing. I saw the bloody horse on my Mammy's grave and the sweet shop lady lighting the candle for her son who wasn't the full shilling, and all the sadness in the world crowded in and I couldn't bear to see Peter Glaze and the cabbages any more. I turned the TV off and went to my room to pray for Mammy in Purgatory-Maybe and Anthony in Limbo-Perhaps, and Mum in mourning and Daddy who needs consolation. And I remembered Father Sullivan and I said 'poor suffering humanity' and that made me feel even sadder.

They listened to his heart. Little – less – nothing! – and that ended it.

When the baby died he was six weeks old but Mum had never held him and that is so sad for her, but what is sadder, and what I can't think about, because it is unthinkable, is that little Anthony never felt his Mammy's arms around him. In all that time he never felt his Mammy's kiss or his Daddy's touch. I wonder if he knew he was loved? Even I loved him and I didn't even see him until he was dead. Cystic fibrosis. They had taken out one of his lungs because his little heart was wrong and it was so hard for him to breathe, but still he died. Even after cutting into his tiny body and taking out a lung, and giving him all that pain which he couldn't even understand because he didn't even have any words yet, he died. His life's little day was just a breath, a tiny moment, but to him, all alone in that incubator thing, it must have seemed for ever, day after day, not understanding why or when or anything about the world and all the people around him. Unheld. It is the worst thing I can imagine.

I have been held. I just can't remember it. I imagine it instead.

I'm never going to watch *Crackerjack* again. I told God that I'd give up *Crackerjack* and *Blue Peter* for ever if he'd just let Anthony know that he's loved. Or go back in time and let Mum hold him. Or just, for God's sake, go back in time and sort the whole bloody thing out. Bloody buggering thing, I said. And then I said it again because it made me feel a bit better. I said what Dad says when Mr Wilson comes on the TV 'Get your finger out.' only I said 'Get your buggering finger out, God.' and because there was no one else in the house I said it out loud. I knew there wouldn't be a thunderbolt or anything but I still sort of waited for one. Holding my breath.

That was hours ago and Mum and Dad are back and I can hear them talking, his rumble and her mumble, and it's still light outside but I'm in my bed. I'll not be able to go to Communion tomorrow with those 'buggers' and 'bloodys' on my soul. Bugger. And Mum will want to know why I'm not going to Communion.

I'll just have to faint again. Fuck it.

They listened to his heart. Little – less – nothing! –
and that ended it.
No more to build on there.
And they, since they
Were not the one dead, turned to their affairs.

DO YOU LIKE KIPLING?
I DON'T KNOW, I'VE
NEVER KIPPLED

Dad's decided I should learn the violin and I couldn't think of a good reason why not, so we borrowed one from the school for ten shillings and I had to go into the music room, which is just a class room with a piano and a music stand, every Tuesday lunchtime and miss recreation completely.

The music teacher, Madam Agnes, was straight off convinced that I could read music. I kept telling her that I couldn't but she didn't hear me. Or I was speaking in some strange language the world doesn't understand.

Dad asked how I was doing so I explained to him that I can't read music and he said that's what the lessons are for, to teach me. So the next Tuesday I told Madam Agnes that I couldn't read music all over again and she just said 'Oh, you'll soon remember it.' And I said 'No, I have never learned' and she said 'Let's start with page eight, 'Au Claire De La Lune'. The only time I remember having a music lesson was in Cyprus in infant school when we sat on a shiny floor singing about a cat and there were notes on a blackboard. The teacher said we weren't trying and we couldn't go home until we really tried. I could see the gardener opening the gate for the mums and dads to come in and collect us and I saw Mammy and I was desperate to go so I started singing as loud as I could, as loud as my lungs would let me. And the teacher stopped playing the piano and said I had to stand in the corner.

I can remember seeing Mammy but I can't remember what she looked like. I wish I could.

But anyway, as well as being a complete disaster in Maths, I could see I was going to be a total disgrace in Violin. It's sort of the same but in a very different way. I worked out straight away that the notes go up and down on the bars from low to high and that all made perfect sense. Then Madam started on the strings, G,D,A and E and I thought 'So far so good.' But then I could feel myself sort of fading away in my brain. Just like Maths, I could do so much, so far, but I could never see why anything is as it is. I stare at the blackboard and nod when Mrs Stringer looks at me, and sometimes I make a wild guess and if it's right, or nearly right, Mrs Stringer is all smiles and says 'Well done, Lucy! You surprised yourself there, didn't you?' And we all know it's supposed to make me feel better, which it doesn't. But Madame Evangelista says I might not have to do Maths next term, which would be lovely, and I can sit and read instead which Dad says is a mark of my bloody idiocy. But even idiots, it seems, should be able to play the bloody violin. Madam Agnes kept tapping the music and saying 'Look! Look!' And I looked and looked but it didn't help, the black blobs had tails or they didn't have tails and they were on the lines or they were off them and it was all nonsense. Dad saw me going to school one morning, because he had to go to court in Devizes and was leaving late, and it was Tuesday. He stopped in the doorway and looked at me and looked so happy, and he said 'Look at my daughter, the convent schoolgirl, with her violin.'

The ten shillings for the violin came out of my money box, the money I buy Mammy's candles with.

Mrs Ash, who is my favourite teacher, said that we must always always tell someone if we don't understand something.

She said that if we don't we just look foolish but if we ask we look interested and interesting. And she told us about the boy who said he had never Kippled. Beth didn't get it but I did because I've read 'Rikki Tiki Tavi' and then lots of other Kipling stories and I started on his poems which are big and brave and soldierly. I do miss the Army, almost as much as I miss my Mammy. I can go whole great lumps of time without thinking about her, but I still miss her all the time. I can't explain that, but it's true.

No one seems to understand that there's something wrong with my brain, no matter how much I ask or tell or don't tell or don't understand. I told Mrs Ash what the doctor said about my Eleven Plus and me being an anomaly but she just said the world was full of them and all the better for it. She said my essays are a beacon of hope for her which doesn't really help.

Next year Mrs Ash will be our form teacher if we stay in the W stream, which I will. Some of the girls are going into 2Y because they've done well in Maths and Science. When you're good at English and RE like me, you stay in the W stream, which is a very happy outcome because we will be Mrs Ash's girls. Beth is quite good at Maths but not so great at other things so she'll be going into 2W with me. Phew.

If I told someone every time I didn't understand something, I'd be in that special hospital for the children who are like me, Educationally Subnormal. I mostly keep quiet about it, but in violin lesson I couldn't pretend. There was no way of pretending. So I had an idea. At first I thought about dropping my violin on the railway under the train but then we'd just have to pay for it and there would be ructions. Mum would have a field day. So, that was a bad idea but the good one came when I nearly caught my shoe bag in the train door and I pulled it out of the way just in time and I thought 'My hand!' If I could catch my hand in the train door, which is very heavy and made of iron or something, I wouldn't be able to play the violin.

Russ Conway has the top of a finger missing but it doesn't stop him playing the piano, so it has to be more than a finger. When Mrs Thingey from 1Y took us for Biology when our teacher was ill, she was going on about the difference between us and monkeys and apparently it's our thumbs. Disposable. Without them we're useless. So actually they're not disposable. They're the very opposite. Undisposable thumbs.

I thought it would be quite an easy thing to do, some hope! The first time I tried, I held back on the platform so I'd be able to slam the door shut behind me, but Mary pushed me ahead of her. The second time, I lost my nerve and pulled my hand out of the way at the last moment. The third time I closed my eyes and slammed the big horrible door really hard but just before it closed a man yanked it open and threw his case on and then sort of fell at my feet, all breathless and triumphant.

I nearly gave up, and I wondered about telling Dad that Madam Agnes refused to teach me to read music and it was all a waste of time, but he had looked so happy when he saw me with that violin that I couldn't. A few weeks ago he said he was going to do my long division with me but after five minutes he was so angry Mum said he was going to have a stroke and it would be my fault and he said 'Is she bloody stupid, Norah? Is she a bloody moron?' And I tried to explain that the numbers don't mean anything to me and how D is like four and F is like seven and they look like words, but his hands clenched and unclenched and I didn't see it coming and my head rang and I went sideways and my legs crumpled and my head hit the sideboard and the best china rattled. Mum stepped in front of him and said 'She's better doing it on her own. You sit down and relax.' And he went in to watch *Steptoe and Son* which always puts him in a good mood. Not that he has a lot of bad moods. He doesn't. But I remembered all that and knew I couldn't tell him about the music again, in case he tried to explain it to me and had a stroke, which Mum says I'll give him one day.

The next morning I let Mary get onto the train first and I daw-dled a bit and as the guard put his arm up I pretended to drop my case on the platform so I got on at the very very very last moment and Mary was already sitting down and no one was looking. I'd worked out that it shouldn't be my right hand because then I wouldn't be able to write or draw or anything, and that even if it was my left hand it would still stop the violin lessons.

At first it didn't hurt. It was just like someone had punched my thumb. And then it burst in on me, the bloody agony of that thumb in that door. The sodding door had locked. It hadn't just banged my hand and swung open again, it had bloody locked. I tried to yell but it was a strangled sort of noise and I couldn't yell any more because I couldn't gulp in any air. Mary was unpacking her homework onto the table and I couldn't shout or cry or anything. A woman saw first – she said 'What's wrong?' But I couldn't say. And she said something to a man and he jumped up and ran to the door and said 'It's alright, it's alright.' But it wasn't.

Mary was as white as a sheet when she saw and the man shouted 'Pull the cord! Pull the cord!' but the woman didn't under-stand what he was saying and she grabbed my shoe bag cord, as if that was going to help. The world was going grey and dim and all the colour was seeping out around the edges and I felt sick and some bugger had run my whole hand through with a sword and I thought, just for a second, about Jesus on the cross. 'Eloi, eloi, lama sabacanthi' but then I wanted to be sick so I stopped thinking about Jesus and concentrated on closing my eyes and not vomiting instead. Funny thing was, the pain started in my thumb but it went right up to my neck and my chin. Sharp. Rapier. The man couldn't help because he was very fat and he couldn't get the window down with me in the way, sagging to my knees. The guard came and he let the window down with the strap and that sent a big shock up my whole arm, and then he shouted at everyone to step back and he opened the door in the wind and the fat man grabbed me and pulled me away and the guard shut the door again. And I was on the floor, crying.

No more violin lessons. The doctor says I'll lose the nail and I've broken two bones and it has to be splinted, and I have to take tablets for two weeks and pain killers every night because the stupid guard, who was very kind and actually quite heroic, ran my hand under a cold water tap in the train toilet and it wasn't drinking water and I got an infection. We have to watch my arm and if red lines go up it, following the veins, that means I may go septic and die. Which is quite exciting.

Instead of Gym and Needlework, I sit at the back of the class and read Kipling. So I have Kippled.

BIG FAT SAINTS

It's rained and rained for weeks. It's the wettest autumn ever. When we got on the train yesterday there was lots of excitement and the Sixth Formers said the school might be flooded and we'd probably have to go home again. It was very exciting. The river had already broken its banks in lots of places and we could see whole fields under water from the train. We ran from the station, trying not to whoop and let the side down because the uniform means we're ambassadors for the convent, for the Nuns, the Church and for Christ, and you'd never see Him playing the giddy goat. I love that idea, a giddy goat, but it doesn't belong in the same sentence as Christ so I make a quick apology.

When we got to the bridge on North Parade we could see the water was up over the banks and reaching the Pavilion and just beginning to lap towards our netball courts. That meant it was already over the Rec and Mary said 'Hooray! No hockey!' and we all cheered even though everyone likes hockey. It was sort of the thing to do. Beth was waiting for us on the bridge and we ran down to the bottom of the Pavilion steps and tried to see how fast it was rising, but we couldn't tell.

In Assembly we said special prayers to keep the waters down and the head mistress was very serious and she said that us new girls couldn't know it, but the floods were terrible and every time the Avon flooded there was more than just water there was dirt and mud and filth and the poor nuns had to clear it all up and it could take weeks and disrupt the whole school calendar.

When we went for our milk in the convent yard, Lisa nudged me and we looked up and we could see, all along the windows, candles lit and statues facing out. Not being Catholic Lisa couldn't understand so I explained that the nuns had turned the statues around to face out over the water, and the river, and had lit the candles, so the saints would keep the water down. Some of the statues had their hands up, like they were blessing the water, or blessing the netball courts. Blessing something, anyway.

With my thumb I couldn't do gym and Lisa was excused because she sprained her ankle last week so we hung around the milk crates for a bit. Then we went to look at the water and it had hardly started creeping up the netball courts. Lisa is a boarder and she was desperate for the floods to reach the school because boarders go into the old gym if there's floods and watch films on Madam Evangelista's projector. And eat stuff from the Tuck Shop that they're not usually allowed. I've never had anything from the Tuck Shop but Beth shares her crisps with me so I have really.

I realised, as we looked at the water, that if the school sent the day girls home, I'd have to sit in the house with Mum in the other room, and me at my desk with only Clint and Cliff and Val Doonican for company. And yesterday when I put their shoes back in the hall, I got in the way because Mum was coming down the stairs and I said 'Sorry' and tried to get into the dining room but she grabbed my wrist and squeezed it hard, like she was trying to do a Chinese burn but couldn't. And she whispered something I couldn't hear, but I was scared and couldn't pull away. Then she let go and went into the kitchen. So, I wasn't sure I really wanted the floods to come, not really, but I sort of did too, because it would be exciting. Then I thought that if the water lapped right up to the basilica and the old gym, it might also creep up over the railway track somewhere between Bath and Chippenham and Mary and me would have to spend the night in a village hall with bacon sandwiches and itchy army blankets. Which would be fun.

The corridor where all the statues had been turned around was in the old convent, and it was a very special corridor because it led to the chapel which was beautiful and smelled of incense and holiness. And you got to it by walking past the kitchens where all the old retired nuns pottered about all day, knitting and making tea with ideal milk in huge yellow metal teapots. I've seen them. Lisa says they put the tea bags in with the ideal milk and then pour boiling water on and it tastes like disgusting custard but she's getting to quite like it. First of all we had to sneak stealthily past the kitchens. Hiawatha was with us, and Tonto and Cheyenne, but I couldn't tell Lisa because it's my private thing. But they were there, and we didn't make a sound. Hiawatha keeps turning into a girl in my head which is confusing. I wish MacAuley had called him something else.

We got to the end of the kitchen corridor, which is the boarder's refectory and an ancient old nun came out and smiled at Lisa and said 'Hello, what are you doing?' And Lisa, quick as a flash said 'We have to see the Reverend Mother, Madam' and the old nun sucked in her breath and blessed us, because the Reverend Mother is a difficult woman, and we fled up the stairs trying not to laugh. I whispered to Lisa 'Will she tell?' And Lisa shook her head 'She doesn't know who *she* is, let alone us.' And we tiptoed into the Holy of Holies.

This corridor is the one with the visitor's room for when your parents come to speak to the head mistress, and the Reverend Mother's Study, and the School Office, and of course, at the end, the Chapel. The whole place smells of polish and flowers and that lovely incense. The floor is like glass. And it's as silent as the grave, not even the ticking of a clock.

The first statue is the Sacred Heart of Jesus and I jerk my head to Lisa and she nods and she takes one side and I take the other and we twist it around. It's a bit awkward because of my thumb splint and the big fat bandage. Then I take the candle and put it in front of the statue on the corridor side. We admire it for a moment and then quickly glide on to the next window and Saint Patrick crushing the head of a snake under his bare foot. This one is a bit bigger but we manage it. There's no noise anywhere but we're getting very near the Reverend Mother's room now so I slip up and put my ear to the door, listening. Tonto raises his eyebrows at me and I nod, 'All quiet'. Lisa whispers 'What?' And I whisper 'Nothing' and she whispers 'What are you nodding about?' And I say 'Nothing'. We move on to Saint Francis who is a big heavy bastard of a statue, and it takes all our puff to turn him, but we do. Then we suddenly hear the head mistress saying 'Good morning!' and we jump a thousand miles in the air and grab each other. Then she laughs and keeps on talking and we realise she's in her office, on the phone. Lisa pats her heart and we manage not to snort too much but I'm beginning to want to wee and it's getting terrifying funny so it's all very dangerous. Perilous. The next statue is Saint Joseph of Arimethea and he's not as fat as Saint Patrick but it's awkward because he has a big white lily in his hand and as we turn it the lily hits the window and Lisa goes 'Shit!', which is understandable because she's Protestant, and she tries to push it back. I put a hand up to steady it because it's wobbling but it's my bad hand and it hurts and I whip it back and shove the other hand up but it's too late and Joseph starts to topple, deadly slow. Lisa's eyes are huge and her mouth is open and Joseph's eyes meet mine and he looks a bit indignant as he falls with an earth shattering crash onto the polished floor. For a moment I can't move. Lisa and me look at each other and then we sort of wake up, like an electric shock, and run and run and run.

We fly down the stairs and past the refectory and out of the back door so we don't have to go past the kitchens again and we sort of reel into the rose garden and we collapse there, stuffing our hands in our mouths, half laughing and half terrified and half excited. We stay there for ages, but we can't hear anything and no one comes out after us. When the lesson bell goes we walk back to 1W as if nothing's happened. As if butter wouldn't melt.

That was yesterday. We had lunch and Lisa and me had to try not to look at each other and Beth knew something was going on so we told her and she thought it was magnificent and foolhardy. Like a Hornblower adventure. Or Saint Trinian's, which I have never seen but I've heard all about.

Then it was afternoon assembly and the head mistress came in like a little fat cloud of thunder. Usually afternoon assembly is just a five minute thing and one of the teachers takes it, so we all knew this was Something Big. I nudged Lisa and she pulled a little face and we wondered. And we were right. A terrible wicked thing had happened and someone had made a mockery of everything we believed in. It was not far short of blasphemy. The whole school would stay there, in the hall, standing, until whoever did it owned up. Pounds and pounds of damage had been done. Vandalism. Cruel and thoughtless and sinful vandalism. And blasphemy.

Lisa and me were bright red. I thought any minute everyone in the school would notice us, and our frozen unseeing gaze and the whole hall would recoil from the heat of our squirming bodies and they'd recognise the guilt slathered on our faces and they would KNOW. The only other person who knew was Beth and she was very very still beside me. Joseph of Arimethea was broken beyond repair and he'd taken a great gouge out of the parquet floor, the Reverend Mother's pride and joy. The scar of this terrible deed would be visible for generations to come. We would all stand there, Madam Bernard Xavier promised, until the culprit or culprits owned up. If that didn't happen today then we would all come back into the hall the next morning and stay there all day if necessary. All week, all month, all term. There would be consequences.

I took a breath but Beth squeezed my hand and whispered, 'Don't.' I managed to look at Lisa but she had her eyes closed and she was swaying slightly and I could see she was going to faint. It was terrible.

And then the doors at the back of the hall banged open and Fishface was hurrying towards the stage, her poor long face twisted in worry and nerves, and she was wringing her hands. BX nodded at her and she went up and whispered something in her ear. I thought 'What now? Has Joseph of Arimethea rolled down the bloody corridor and down the stairs and slaughtered the kitchen staff?' But then Fishface was off, running away down the hall and the head mistress said 'Girls, we have been advised to close the school as quickly as we can. If you're a boarder stay where you are for the moment. The roads around the City Centre are in imminent danger of flooding so those of you who have buses and trains to catch, please leave now.' So we did.

I can't remember much except the huge wonderful thank-you-God relief of it. Mary grabbed me in the cloakroom and said 'Come on, let's run' and we did. I ran and ran and ran until I got a stitch and on the North Parade I stopped and leaned on the bridge and laughed and laughed and laughed. Mary said 'What?' And I said 'You wouldn't understand.' but then she looked at me, and went all quiet and she said 'You... you didn't?'

And I said 'What? No.' But she shook her head at me and said

'Lucy Gannon, you'll end up in prison, you will.' Which I think may be true.

So, here I am, at home, stuck at my rotten table which I have to call a desk, pretending to do homework and I wish I was at school. The floods are terrible, all over Somerset but especially in Bath. It's on the news, old grannies in rowing boats and babies being born on roofs and everything.

And I know who's to blame.

Let the stormy clouds chase
Everyone from the place
Come on with the rain
I've a smile on my face
I walk down the lane
With a happy refrain
Just singin',
Singin' in the rain .

TOGETHER LET US
EXPLORE THE STARS

Christmas was OK. Mostly. I hadn't got any money to buy Christmas presents so I made special cards for everyone. Mum's card was easy, flowers and a rainbow but I didn't know what to do for Dad so I ended up drawing a monstrance, a pipe and a bottle of wine. He laughed when he saw it but it was a pleased sort of laugh and he said 'An ostensorium!' and I said 'No, it's a monstrance' and he said that ostensorium is another word for it. I wrote it down in my rough book because it's a lovely word, and I think that must be where we get 'ostentatious' from, but it seems a bit blasphemous. Mum says Mrs Carter's new Ford is ostentatious, which means that the golden vessel that holds the body of Christ is like a white Ford with leopard skin seats. I don't think so. I think she's got that wrong. When Norman came to play chess with Dad he looked at the card and said 'That's you, summed up nicely.' And Dad said 'A gift from my daughter. Well, it's better than a slap in the belly with a wet fish.'

That's the last card I make for him.

Martin sent me a postal order for five pounds. Five pounds! Mum wasn't ecstatic. Peter didn't even write 'And from Master Peter, sweet fanny adams.' Dad said. Mum said you can't say that in front of me because I'm just looking for an excuse, but the whole point of it is that you can't say the other F.A. but you can say Fanny Adams.

Aunty Nelly sent me a transistor radio. My own radio! I'm not allowed to have it in my bedroom at night but if I finish my homework I can have it on in the dining room. It's a Bush Radio and it's pale green and gold and I love it. The best thing is that I can have it on really low, almost too low for the human ear, as I do my homework, and no one knows but me. I listen to Radio Luxembourg which comes and goes and sometimes whines so I have to quickly turn the sound absolutely off, and the American Forces Radio Service, and of course the Light Programme. I love America. When I grow up I am going work on a ranch and marry an American. Everyone's America mad, not just me. The Nuns are in ecstasy about John F. Kennedy becoming the President because he's Irish and Catholic and very handsome. I thought nuns didn't notice if men were handsome but Madam Agnes is in love with Kenneth McKellar and when she plays 'The Scottish Soldier' on the record player in wet rec she holds the LP cover and gazes at his photo and thinks no one notices. We all do. And now all the whole convent is in love with John Kennedy.

When school started again after Christmas, everyone had forgotten all about Joseph of Arimethea, and the only sign of the floods was a strange smell in the basilica, some grit on the netball court and a high tide mark all around the tin hut. The rest of the school was fine because the water had stopped at the Tuck Shop. The first time we went to Chapel for Benediction, along the Holy of Holies corridor, I looked for the dent in the parquet floor and there was a bit of one, but it's not terrible, just a little mark, a tiny scar. It made me smile a bit. A battle scar. We don't have a statue of Joseph of Arimathea any more.

I listen to *Beyond Our Ken* on Saturdays, and so does Beth and on Monday we act out the best bits of the show, and she does Kenneth William's voice and I do all the ladies who are all Betty

Marsden. We try Stanley Unwin but he's quite difficult. I think that the British are best at being funny, but the American's are best at being heroic and romantic. Which is a good reason to marry one. Another good reason is Clint Walker and Richard Chamberlain. I know that the nuns, clearing up after the floods, were heroic too because we have photographs of them. Madam Ignatius has her habit rolled up and tucked in her belt like Father David used to, and Fishface is in huge wellies and her veil is wonky, and BX has the biggest brush you've ever seen and they're ankle deep in slime. So they are heroic, but you can't marry a nun, can you? In the Middle Ages priests used to marry them, and monks did too, but when I told Fishface she wrung her hands and said 'Oh, you're so bold, Lucy Gannon.' Which is a bit rich when I was just saying what it says in a proper history book.

It's 1961 and I'll soon be a teenager, whatever Dad says, and Kennedy is the leader of the world and everyone's talking about the Space Race and who will be the first Nation to have an outpost on the Moon. I'm sure it will be America. This is the most exciting time ever to be alive, because whatever happened in history, whatever age you born into, we are the first generation who can literally reach for the stars. Literally. The Russians have already sent a dog up, which is typical of them. Beth and me have made a promise to each other that one day we will achieve something wonderful, not in Space, maybe just something quiet in a back room boffin sort of way, but something grand, that we will take, quietly and unassumingly, to our graves with pride. It probably won't involve Maths.

When it's a Maths lesson Mrs Stringer doesn't ask me anything and I'm allowed to read a book. Mrs Stringer is perfectly nice to me, even though I'm not in the class properly, and she chats away like she does to everyone and I like her almost as much as Mrs

Ash. Mrs Ash is probably going to be my crush. We all get one, apparently. No one in my form has yet but the whole of 4W is in love with the Head Girl, who is a snotty sort of Enid Blyton sort of person, a villain not a hero. We asked Mrs Ash about crushes, because you can talk to her about anything and she said they were practice runs for falling in love. Christine Tierney, who is as cheeky as all get-out, asked if she was in love with Mr Ash and she laughed and said 'Sometimes' but a few days later she came in furious, and threw her bag down and folded her arms and squared up to all twenty-three of us and said 'Be warned. Do not cross me today. I threw a teapot at Mr Ash this morning and it was a teapot I was very fond of.' Lisa whispered 'Do you think it hit him?' But Mrs Ash heard and she said 'I wish it had. At least then it might not have shattered.' When she gave out the essays she whacked me on the head with mine and said 'twenty-seven ands! Read more! Write less!' Which was a bit unnecessary as she'd given me nine out of ten. She says that in twenty years of marking essays she has never given ten out of ten because there is no such thing as a perfect essay. There is always always room for improvement.

I don't see how I can read any more than I do. I've finished every single book by Georgette Heyer and all the Agatha Christie ones, and Daddy's *Treasury of English Poetry* that he got as a prize at the seminary and everything else I can lay my hands on.

Mrs Ash said that Georgette Heyer is better than nothing, but only just, and she's going to bring in some books from home because she says the school library is pious and deadly. We didn't know if she really meant that or if it was just her mood, with the teapot. Our teapot is metal. I thought it was silver but Dad said it's electro plated. So Mum can throw it at him any time she likes and it won't break, but of course she won't because they are so very obviously in love, besotted and soul mates. They are so much

in love there is no room for anyone else. If Anthony Gerard had
lived he would be a part of their love, because Dad would love
the bit of him that was Mum and Mum would love the bit of him
that was Dad. I'm not sure if Daddy ever loved my Mammy like
that. I think if he did, he might go all misty eyed like in the films
where the Daddy says to the little girl 'You remind me of your
Mother.' but he never does.

Mum did that wrist thing again, twice. She squeezes as hard
as she can and her eyes pop and she whispers. The third time she
did it I was ready and I was listening and what she said was
'Loathsome. Loathsome.' Which is a bit rich, even for her.

My thumb is almost back to normal now and yesterday I
played hockey for the first time since the splint came off. I was
going to play hockey, anyway. On the way down to the Rec, running across the old netball court, the one we don't use any more,
there were all these stones lying around from the floods and we
were whacking them. Beth was just in front of me because she's
small and fast and I'm big and quite slow, and she took this huge
swing at a stone and the hockey stick hit it and kept on swinging
and it went high up, and over her shoulder and it hit me in the
nose. It's broken. The hospital said it was concussion and I'm not
to run or bend down quickly. Daddy took one look and started
laughing. Mum was not amused. My head hurts like billy-oh and
it's quite nice going to bed even earlier than usual and drawing
the curtains and lying here with William Tell, hiding from the
swinish Gessler.

I know what Aunty Nelly will say when she reads my letter,
she'll say 'If it's not her arse, it's her elbow.'

I feel as if something huge is going to happen. Beth says it's
the New Year that's doing it, but that was weeks ago. I go into
Mary's house sometimes on the way home from the train and

Mum doesn't notice if it's just five minutes or so. When I told Mary's Mum that I thought something tremendous was going to happen she went all spooky and said 'Show me your hand' and she traced the lines and said 'I can tell you that something very wonderful is going to happen very soon.' And I said 'What?' And she said 'It will appear behind you and it will be just what the doctor ordered' and then someone laughed and I turned around and Mary was there with a lovely coconut sponge her Mammy had baked. We ate it all and I didn't tell Mum.

The house is a silent house. They stop talking when I walk into a room now so I don't walk in on them unless I really have to, and I hate apologising for interrupting because it's childish and it isn't true anyway. I'm not sorry. But it's a rule that I have to say it, so I do. Like if they're watching telly I have to knock first because it's their time, not mine. I suppose I am sorry in a way, sorry that I have to say sorry, sorry I have to walk in and speak, sorry they're in the room and that I am in the house. On Friday I realised that in three whole days I hadn't even spoken to Mum and she hadn't spoken to me. Daddy still doesn't realise it. Maybe he does but he just doesn't want to. It's like the Cinderella story when Baron Hardup is so in love with the step mother that he never sticks up for Cinders. But I'm not Cinders. I'd like to write an essay about how a pantomime can actually say something really truthful but I don't know how to put it into a story. And Mrs Ash might think I'm writing about me. Which would be mortifying and shameful. Who would ever admit that they aren't loved because they aren't loveable? Not me. I would never ever ever admit that to anyone.

My Baron Hardup really is in love with his new wife. Newish. He is passionate. You can see it. It makes me happy and sad at the same time. I can't remember him being passionate with my Mammy but then, I don't remember my Mammy at all, so maybe he was. I hope so. But hoping in the past tense is impossible. It just becomes something else, like longing. I long for him to have loved my Mammy. I wonder if you can pray for something in the past tense? Well, obviously you can, but I wonder if it works? If God's eternal like they say, then it should.

I can't wait for the day when I walk away from Orchard Crescent, Chippenham. I will never come back. Never. I have nearly five pounds in my money box now but I'm not allowed to spend it. It's for a rainy day. I imagine that day, when it's pouring down and the roads are flooded and I'm walking away from Mum and the fish knives and the to-do list and the weeding. I'm walking through great streams of floods, my feet sploshing, my head down, but there's money in my pocket and I'm making my way steadily and stubbornly to Newton Le Willows, to buy a dozen roses and some bright yellow daffodils, to put on Mammy's grave. Everyone says that sometimes I'm very morbid but the funny thing is, when I've done the whole journey up to Mammy's grave in my head, and I'm there at the grave side, and the flowers are in the vase Aunty Nelly bought, I do this great big V sign to Mum and Dad and I feel wonderful, like I've really done it. Like doing it in my head means something, and a great bubble seems to rise up in my soul and I laugh, all by myself up here in my lilac bedroom, I laugh and I do V signs and V signs and V signs.

I still feel as if something wonderful is going to happen. It's a great big new brave world, and the President of the United States is a handsome Catholic man from Ireland, and it seems that I'm quite good at English when before I was good at absolutely nothing, so even though my bedroom is lilac, the future is just wonderful. Everyone's future. My future. My generation.

BLESS ME FATHER,
FOR I HAVE SINNED

Something huge happened but it wasn't wonderful. It was terrible. Something terrible, awful, catastrophic happened last week. I am changed for ever. I don't really want to think about it any more but I have because next Saturday I'll have to confess it.

I've never bought anything from the Tuck Shop because I never have any money. I can't keep on taking Beth's crisps and a bite of Lisa's Wagon Wheel but they don't want me to just sit there without anything every rec time. I shouldn't want to eat anything, being such a fat little thing, and I get all that I need, and more, at mealtimes, according to the Baron Hardup's new wife. Newish. The sight of me offends her and all I can think is 'You're very bloody easily offended then,' but then I feel guilty and I hate her but I hate me even more. Anyway, it's been really filling my head, that Tuck Shop. The smell of the crisps and the crunch and the crinkle of the paper. Fishface runs it but it's beyond her really, and she gets all flustered because the girls are always starving and they elbow each other out of the way and panic that the bell's going to go for end of break. It's like a jumble sale, like we had in Golborne where Peter got me that pen with the floating naked lady and Aunty Nelly slapped my legs for it.

I was waiting for Beth and she was waiting in the queue, with Fishface shouting at everyone, and the Fifth Formers leading her a merry dance. It was going to take for ever so I wandered off to the basilica and sat on one of the changing benches and there was this purse. A school purse. The zip was open and I could see a ten shilling note.

So stupid, so stupid, so stupid. I am so stupid. And now wicked as well. Criminal. Loathsome. I shoved it in my blouse pocket and then I could feel my face burning and I was going all jerky and strange so I went to the loo. I thought 'What if they search everyone?' so I shoved it down my sock. When I came home I hid it in my Missal, in the cover, but even that was the wrong thing to do, like hiding it in a Bible, or shoving it in Christ's pocket. Everyone knows I never have money, everyone knows I can never go to Maynard's Sweet Shop on the way home. What was I going to do? I couldn't even buy candles for Mammy because it's tainted money.

I was desperate to think about something else on the train but I couldn't. Mary kept asking what was wrong and I couldn't tell her. I kept wondering if the ten shillings belonged to Katherine with the TB Mum and was it meant to buy flowers for her? I could see Katherine, down the carriage, and I tried to hear if she was talking about someone stealing her money but she was just laughing and going on about homework. 'Stealing'. I am a thief. On top of everything else.

When I got home that night there was nothing to do but think about it, no one to talk to, no one to watch, nothing but me and the stripey wallpaper and the sounds of the TV in the next room. People talking, noble normal people, not hopeless thieves. I could hardly swallow the boiled egg and the Kia Ora tasted like iron and I felt so sick. I prayed and prayed but I couldn't get through to anyone. I did my homework but I can't even remember what it was. I didn't turn on the tranny, as a sort of penance.

Then I just lay in my bed, under the crucifix, and I couldn't look at it and I couldn't even pray for my Mammy, just lay there in a great cloud of nothing. Nihilism. I read about it in ... oh, who cares? Somewhere.

My head was so jumbled I couldn't even think about Clint or Perry or anyone. Couldn't escape seeing that ten shilling note. I even thought I could smell it, a musty old paper smell. Filling my lilac bloody room. I knew Dad would never forgive me if I was found out and Mum, well Mum, I couldn't even think of that. She'd be on her high horse, whinnying with delighted shock, so she would. I wanted to die. I just wanted to die. Better that than be expelled. I didn't think I'd sleep, but I did and the very first thought when I woke up was 'Did that really happen?' But it did. The damn ten shillings is still there.

On the way, in the train, I rested my head against the window and watched the rain drops chasing down and I knew what I had to do, and I wanted to die.

It was Maths so no one would miss me. The Holy of Holies corridor was just the same as it always is. The silence there makes everything feel slow and dreamy and sacred. That and the polish. I knocked on Madam Bernard Xavier's door and when she called out 'Come in' I nearly ran. But I didn't. I walked in. She looked surprised. I walked right up to the desk and put the ten shilling note on it and said 'I stole it. I'm sorry.' She looked at it and then at me and then she said, very calmly 'Who did you steal it from?' And I said 'I don't know, Madam, just a purse in the basilica,' and she nodded and said 'Thank you, Lucy. You can go back to your lessons now.'

And that was it. I couldn't believe it. I spent all the rest of the day waiting to be called to The Reverend Mother's Study, or to be marched off the premises or something but nothing happened. Nothing.

That was on Wednesday. On Friday Mrs Ash asked me to stay behind after our Form Lesson and I thought 'This is it. I'm expelled.' And she said that BX had written to Dad and Mum and asked them to come in and see her. BX, not Mrs Ash. In the first World War men felt their insides turn to water, before they went over the top, and that's what happened to me. Gallons of liquid shite roiling around in my belly and I went hot and cold at the same time. I felt like crying and Mrs Ash said, quite quickly, 'It's not about anything you've done.' And the way she said it, sort of nudge-nudge wink-wink meant she knew about the ten bob. She said again 'It *really* isn't about *anything* you've done, Lucy, so there is nothing to worry about. The head mistress wanted you to know that.' And that was it. Again. I was very confused.

Dad wasn't happy about having to go into Bath on a Saturday morning and Mum kept asking me what it was about and I kept saying I didn't know, and I really didn't. I couldn't work it out. She kept asking me what I'd done, had I been rude? Had I failed some exam, but I told her there weren't any exams and I didn't know. I didn't go with them. I stayed at home and listened to my radio which should have been a wonderful treat but I couldn't really hear it, because I was so worried. And then I thought that maybe they would send me back to Aunty Nelly and that would be even worse than this but at least there would be Aunty Nelly and I'm big enough now to stop the other thing, amn't I? I think I might be. But then I remembered his thick brown arms and the smell of him and I'm not sure, but the thought of Aunty Nelly…
.. So I started to hope that BX would tell them everything and that Dad would be so furious he would march me to the station and put me on a train. Or that Mum would grab my wrist and squeeze so hard it would break and I'd be sent away to recuperate. Or she'd kill me and get it over with. I think one day she might.

When they came back, they were very quiet. Mum went into the garden and started mowing the lawn like she was killing the grass, murdering it blade by blade, blood dripping from her eyes. Dad called me into the front room. The nuns had said I was a very good girl and a credit to the school and to him. I stared at him. I couldn't believe it and neither could he, but he pretended that he could. I call him The Great Pretender. No, I don't. Concentrate.

The nuns said I was doing very well but they had noticed that I never had any tuck money or money for sweets or treats or anything like that. And that made me the odd one out. They said I should have pocket money. So, I'm getting sixpence a day! Sixpence a day! Five school days, six pence daily, that's a half crown every week. Then he asked, carefully like the words were hurting him 'Have you told anyone that you are unhappy?' And I said no, of course not. He asked me if I ever talked about home to the teachers and I said no, because Mum had said I must never talk about home to anyone. And he looked a little bit sad. I thought he might ask me if I *was* unhappy and I panicked a little bit because I didn't know what I'd say. But he didn't. Of course he didn't.

When Mum came in she couldn't bear to look at me and when she put the dinner on the table she said 'Make the most of it, there'll be no lamb next week. Half crowns don't grow on trees.' But I don't care, from now on I'll have money that I'm allowed to spend, but more than that. It all means more than that. It means that I'm not invisible. I'm not sure what it means, but it means something. Maybe that I'm not entirely exactly alone. That the nuns know. That what it is, here in this house, isn't right. That maybe it's not all me that's wrong, maybe it's her as well. And him.

Cheyenne gives me a crooked smile, and Dr Kildare pats my hand, and Perry says 'We all make mistakes, Della.' And Della smiles and tip-taps away to bring us cawfee. I still have to get through confession and I hope it's not Father Sullivan or he'll never be able to see me without thinking 'thief'. But I hope it is Father Sullivan too, in a way, because he'll be lovely. I wish I hadn't taken the bloody thing. But I'm glad I did because now I'm getting pocket money. I'm very confused.

Bless me father for I have sinned. I stole ten shillings but I took it back. Ah, so not so much stole as borrowed, then? I suppose so, Father. Good girl, Lucy.

How does he always know it's me?

One thing I know now, for sure, I am not a hero. No one will ever carve my name with pride. Another thing I know, when I get my first crush, I think it may be on Madam Bernard Xavier. Or Father Sullivan. Actually, I think maybe I've had a crush or two or three for years. I think maybe that's what Clint has been about, and Hoss and all the others.

I think it may be sex, rearing its ugly head.

WHERE THE HEELS
COME FROM

Dad watches the News all the time, and when it's not on the TV he can usually find some on the radio, or he reads the paper. Sometimes he has the radio on at the same time as the TV. Like there won't be anything happening in the world unless he, Gerard Anthony Gannon is au fait with it all. Normally it's just tax and budgets but that's all changed. Russia is building missile launching pads in Cuba, which is just a hop away from America and JFK says that they will all be pointed at Florida, and could reach much further into the heartlands of the USA. I'm trying to grow out of my day dreams and think more about Cuba and less about the ridge where the West commences. It's called growing up, which I don't want to do, but short of topping myself there's no option. Peter Pan and all that.

A woman from the WRVS came to tell us what to do if the four minute warning sounds. This means that we will have four minutes to take shelter from the atomic fallout. We all thought that if Cuba fired at America we would be too far away to worry, although we would be upset and angry of course and be dragged, reluctantly, into the fray. That's what Dad says. It turns out that America has troops here and as soon as Cuba fires on the USA, these troops, and probably our Army and Airforce, will attack Russia. Russia will then, probably, bomb the American troops in this country and if they do that with atomic weapons we will all be Wiped Out. If any missiles are launched, our radar will see them and someone will start the sirens and we will have four minutes to hide.

The WRVS woman said that we must tape around our windows so that the radio active dust doesn't seep in, and we must not, on any account, turn to look at the blast. She told us to tell our parents to make sure we had candles, tinned goods, bottled water and some house bricks. The house bricks are so that we can put them around a candle in a jam jar and make a stove on which we can heat baked beans and even, if we're not in a hurry, boil water. We should draw all the curtains and take shelter under a table and stay there until the radio tells us that it's safe to go out again.

She talked to the whole school in the hall, and all the teachers came and sat at the end of our rows. Someone asked her where our nearest Army base was, because that's what the Russians would be firing at and she didn't know. I chirped up 'Warminster. And the whole of Salisbury Plain is an Army training area.' A First Former started crying because it's only a few miles away. I said that what was even more worrying was that the Army had a lot of armoured units on the plain, tanks and armoured vehicles and all sorts, and the School of Infantry and a whole load of laboratories where they were working on neutralising chemical weapons, so the Russians were bound to go for them. My Dad had been stationed there so I knew, for sure. Some other girls started crying and another first former said her Daddy was in Salisbury and she didn't want him to die. Beth said 'Don't be daft, our tanks will shoot the bomb down before it lands' and that cheered her up a bit. I was going to point out that this wouldn't help because the damn thing would still explode but before I could, Beth said her Dad could work a Bofors gun and they can shoot down anything, and they probably had them on the top of the Admiralty Building on The Parade. Now everyone was asking us questions instead of the WRVS lady and she clapped her hands and said maybe we should go back to talking about the present crisis and something about cool heads diverting disaster. Beth told everyone about the time the Army transport plane taking me and Mammy out to join the Regiment at Cyprus crash landed at Orly airport and how we had all remained calm and slightly heroic. She said that was a case of wise heads. She got some of it wrong so I told the story again, how all the Mums didn't believe us children when we told them the wing was on fire and my Mammy saying 'Yes, OK, we heard you the first time. Finish your colouring in.' And how the Captain came on the loudspeaker and said that an engine was on fire and how all the Mums felt really stupid. And how there were great streams of ambulances and fire engines racing along beside us as we landed. All that. I told them about going down the big emergency chutes, like slides, but I don't think that bit really happened. It just made it all a bit more exciting. When I finished everyone clapped. Miss Campbell told me to sit down and button it. She is very tall and smart and always says things like 'button it.' She wears one turquoise stocking and one purple one some- times, and very short skirts and huge glasses and she's our Art teacher. She is the epitome of glamour. I said that to Mrs Ash and she said it's epitomy not epitome. She bestrides the corridors like a colossus and I think Beth might have an embryonic crush developing.

Before I buttoned it, I asked the lady what we would do if we were on the train when the siren sounded and she didn't know. She said that someone would give us instructions. Mary rolled her eyes and whispered 'Because the guard has a direct phone connection with the White House, je ne sais pas.' and we got the giggles. Mrs Ash gave us a hard look. A girl in 4X asked if it was true we'd bleed from every orifice if we got fallout sickness but the lady didn't know that either. Someone asked her where our orifices were and that was it, we were off, in total hysterics. Mrs Ash, completely unamused, said we'd asked enough questions as the lady had other schools to visit. The lady said we were all very lively. Une euphemism, je pense.

In our Form Lesson Mrs Ash said we could talk about our worries if we wanted to, but we didn't have to. What did we want to do? No one said anything, and they all just looked at each other, so I put my hand up and said that I had lived in Ulster where everyone wanted to bomb us all the time, and in Egypt where they had tried to kill my Daddy, where we went to school in an Army truck with a machine gun on the roof and soldiers guarding us, and in Cyprus where the Greeks hated the Turks and everyone hated us, and I'd been spat at and had stones thrown at me, but here I was, thirteen years old and still alive and kicking. Just. Lisa said 'Worse luck' and we talked about the netball tournament instead.

That night, when I finished my homework, I knocked the door and went into the front room and told Dad what we had to do, the bricks and everything, but he just pulled a face and said 'No bloody chance. If we're going up, we're going up.' And then he turned back to the TV. I looked at Mum but she was knitting a sock and turning a heel so she didn't even have to pretend to look at me, concentrating.

I'm worried about Aunty Nelly and wonder if she knows about the four minute thing, so I write to her and buy a stamp off Mum and she says she'll post it at the main Post Office, so it'll get there quickly. Sometimes she can be really nice, and utterly amazing, but she still doesn't look at me.

Four minutes is hardly anything at all, and it makes you a bit wary about going to the toilet. Knowing my luck I'll be right in the middle of my business when we all go up. Which is what Dad says will happen, but the WRVS woman said it will be a new beginning and Madam Celine said that God will be looking after us. These nuns are such innocents. She says that Mr Kennedy will keep the world safe, but Dad says JFK is a tailor's dummy and a rich boy, and he only cares about America, and he doesn't even care about that much. I think he cares a lot because he said *"The cost of freedom is always high – but Americans have always paid it. And one path we shall never choose, and that is the path of surrender or submission."*

The world is holding its breath.

I think she was talking rubbish, that woman. If you could protect yourself with a table and some sellotape and a candle, it's not much of a weapon, is it? Either it's a complete failure as bombs go, or she's got it all wrong and Dad's right and we're teetering at the edge of the end of the world. It's a bit of an insult really, all the candle and bricks stuff, when you think how many thousands and thousands died in Japan at the end of the war. They'd have been alright under a kitchen table? I don't think so. Little Japanese babies are still being born with stunted limbs and all sorts.

The only way a brick and a candle would be any good would be if you were actually standing behind the man with his finger on the button, and then you could stove his head in. Knowing my luck, instead of heroically averting total catastrophe, I'd smack him so hard and at exactly the wrong moment so that he'd fall slap bang onto the button, with his whole head, and then the world would end and it would be all my fault. And all them candles and bricks would be redundant. That's what Madam Celine says about my jokes 'Your wit is redundant, Lucy Gannon.' Beth says that hers is non-existent. Beth is an atheist and she says lots of things are non-existent. I told her about nihilism and she said she likes the sound of that.

She also says that thirteen is too young to die but you can die at any time, it comes like a thief in the night, a bullet from a sniper, an arrow from a bow, and there's nothing you can do about it. Mammy was forty something, which makes me a late child, and Anthony was just six weeks. Beth hasn't had anyone die on her yet, so she doesn't realise it can just happen, just like that. I hope that, if it does all end, I'm at school with all my friends and Mrs Ash. But I don't think anyone in the world is stupid enough to press the button on the Atomic Bomb.

Famous last words. Wouldn't it be funny if those were my last words? Not Funny Ha-ha, Funny Peculiar. Me sitting here at the table pretending to be a desk, Cheyenne making paper planes, Perry Mason reading case notes by my side, and Cilla Black singing 'Step Inside Love'. What a way to go.

CHRISTMAS BLOODY CHRISTMAS

We're still here. It was all so much hot air. We're still in Chippenham, which is the longest I've ever lived anywhere, and Uncle Alf is dead. I didn't even go to his funeral. I would have been tempted to do a jig on his grave. I've not seen Aunty Nelly for three years. Even if I tried I couldn't have squeezed out a tear for Uncle Alf, although everyone should be wept for, even Hitler. Maybe not Hitler. Most people. I can't cry for my Mammy any more either, or even for Aunty Nelly. I am chronically dry eyed.

Martin's due home from Borneo in January but then he's off again to British Guiana which is on the other side of the world. He says he'll have two weeks with us and Mum says 'Oh, he will, will he?' And Dad says quietly 'Yes, he will.' And she goes pink.

In RE last week we had a visit from Canon Someone, from Somewhere. Probably Prior Park but I don't know. Anyway, he had a voice like a bee on a summer's day and it gave me a tingly neck and all I wanted to do was close my eyes and sleep. It's lovely when it's like that but you daren't close your eyes because if you did your head would jerk and everyone would laugh. Or worse, you'd snore and wake yourself up like Judith did in Mass. He said that if you even think something, you've as good as done it. It's not a new idea but I realised that if it's true it means I've killed Mum and set fire to her bloody precious Wilton carpet every week for the last year. It's new and it has to last twenty years. So,

I've killed her fifty-two times, at least. And become an arsonist.
There is no end to my talent. Which is what Iggy, Madam Ignatius
says, but she's not being sarcastic, she's just being Iggy. There's
a rumour that she was married before she came to the convent but
I don't quite believe it. But if any of the nuns was going to be a
married woman once, and maybe even a Mum, I'd say it was her.
She isn't Irish, she's a Londoner and she says things like 'Oy, put
a sock in it.' And 'Pack it in, you raucous crew – you're giving
me ear ache.' She's lovely.

The tingly neck thing is lovely too and Beth says it's what
happens when you do sex. But she's not got that right. I get a
tingly neck when I think about Jesus and in Benediction and
sometimes in the Mass. I keep thinking about Jesus. Everyone else
pales into insignificance next to Him. I wrote that phrase in an
essay about the space race last week and Mrs Ash said it would
have been very apt if I didn't spell 'pale' like 'pail'. Not as bad as
Beth though, who wrote that the soul of Odysseus hoovered in the
afterlife. That made us all laugh. Anyway, we were talking about
how Christ was a prophet unrecognised in His own country and
all that, and I told Fishface that the convent statues are all wrong
because Christ was a Jew in the Middle East so even if he wasn't
small and wiry and brown, with a hooked nose like lots of Arabs,
then he was pale skinned and blue eyed but not like we are, like a
white Arab who looks different from us, and she went very pink
and flustered 'Stop it! Just stop it, Lucy Gannon.' I told her I saw
lots of people like that in Egypt and she said Israel isn't Egypt and
stop being so perverse, and Leanne said that Israel didn't exist in
Jesus's time and Fishface said it did – what about Bethlehem? I
told her my Dad said it was all a terrible mistake after the war and
some eedjit in Whitehall drew up a new country and you couldn't
do that to people and Lisa chimed in with 'Israel was the Jewish

race in the Bible, not a place at all', but she's a Protestant, so she doesn't properly know anything. Catherine, who is also a Prottie, but wants to be a Catholic more than anything, told her to shut up and it all got noisy and chaotic and a bit too much for Fishface who was nearly crying by this time, and she stamped her foot which made us all laugh. I do love it when the whole class goes off on one like that. And then we felt mean so we helped her to pack up the Tuck Shop.

Anyway, Jesus isn't someone you could fancy, but He was pure love, and deserving of our respect, whatever He looked like. The way He worried about His mother's grief, in the middle of His own agony, and gave her into the care of John. And I like everything He says and how He doesn't bugger around being polite when people are stupid but how kind He is when they're in trouble, like the leper. Even the woman who bled for twelve years, which must have been awful when they had to make do with rags like Mum did when she was a girl, and who would have been properly outcast by all the Jews, ritual bathing and all that, but not by Him. He went out of his way to find people that no one else could stand. The unloved. Which is heroic all on its own even before He died. Beth says I'm in love with Him but He's a bit more deserving than Karen Wills, the tennis Captain, who she completely adores. Dad says you shouldn't give God a capital H but I think you should. He also says you don't need to cross yourself when a funeral passes, but there's no medical way of knowing when a dead person's soul goes up to Heaven so maybe they're there, seeing you going about your business, not a care in the world. Which would be hurtful. It could be someone's Mammy in that coffin, or someone's little brother. And anyway, what's so terrible about crossing yourself, even if it's a waste of time? Better safe than sorry.

I think about Christ more and more. I'm not sure if it's praying. I hope He knew, when He was alive, maybe even while He was being crucified, that here we would be, two thousand years later, still properly loving Him. I think that would have been a comfort when he was in Gethsemane or walking towards Calvary, falling under the weight of the cross. In Science we talked about time and space and although physics haven't found a way yet, time machines are a scientific possibility, as our understanding of space improves. I said 'It's just a matter of time.' but no one got it except me and Beth. I'm wasted here.

I've grown out of the dying thing. I think it was all about Mammy and not really about dying at all. I know now that you can't slow down your metabolism so much that you die. That's what I was trying to do, although I didn't know about metabolism at the time.

Funny that I didn't know about it but I still knew about it all the same. I think I might be tempted to have a better go at it one day, a rope or something a little more likely to work, like jumping off Beachy Head (which is a real possibility because the Donaghues live there and we go down every month) but just now it's sort of OK. Mum and me don't spend any time in the same room and I'm getting used to it while Dad pretends he hasn't noticed. I try not to think about Mammy too much, but I still say the Rosary for her, just in case Purgatory exists. There was a boy in Chippenham called that. Justin Case. Or I might have made it up. Sometimes I think things and then I can't remember if they're true or not. I dream that I'm waiting to be decapitated in some Middle Eastern palace, and the dream is so real that I know what it's like to wait, hopeless and empty, for execution in a cold marble corridor, where the only sound is the gentle slap of sandals behind a closed door and the chink of a tea cup. I know what it feels like to be there, when your heart is hammering in your ears, dizzy with fear and dread, counting the minutes, the breaths, wondering if I'll sob and wail and grab onto the shiny cold floor, trying to dig my fingernails in, as they drag me away. I wake up before they come for me.

I dream it again on Christmas Eve so that in the morning I feel a bit sick, and my head aches, but it's Christmas and I have to take Communion at the ten o'clock Mass so it's just sweet tea in the tiny dining room as silent as any marble palace. The Communion wafer has to go into an empty stomach but I don't see why, it goes through all the other bits of me and it doesn't come out in a nice white holy state, does it? Anyway, anyway, Mum and me sit there, smiling like dolls, while Dad has poached eggs because he never takes Communion. No one says anything so I think about what's in the parcels under the Christmas tree. Then I think what Mrs Ash would give me if I was her little girl, which is something I'd quite like really, and I think she'd probably give me a really good book, or three or four. I've saved some of my sixpences whenever I could resist the Tuck Shop, and I'm giving Dad an EP of Vivaldi. I didn't have enough for Mum's Apple Blossom perfume so I got her the talcum powder. Dad would really like Bach's *Mass in B Minor* which is a double album and Mum would really like me gone, so no one will get their heart's desire this year. We smile again and pretend that we will.

It's not Father Sullivan saying Mass and I wonder if he's gone home to see his Mammy, who has stones in her gall bladder, which sounds like something Biblical, like Lot's wife. Father Sullivan says it's very common but terrible painful and he does worry about his Mammy. You don't think of a priest being someone's little boy, but he was, and I expect he still is, in his Mammy's heart. No one says 'Mammy' here except him and me. It's nice, and a bit sad too. Mammy Mammy Mammy. So there.

When we get back Mum bastes the turkey, which is huge and sweaty and pink and a bit revolting. Half starved to death we have toast and jam in the kitchen, which is where we never ever eat because there's no room, but we all stand by the sink and try to think of things to say and pretend we can't wait to get to the presents. The turkey's not going to be ready for hours and hours.

I get knickers and a bra, which is really mortifying, and socks, Scrabble and two books – *The Children Of The New Forest*, which I read years ago, and *The Incredible Journey*. By the time the Queen makes her speech, I've read *The Incredible Journey*, cover to cover. Dad and me play Scrabble but he beats me – 260 to 140, although I got the best word, 'zephyr' on a triple word square, and he tried not to be surprised. If I ever do anything even half clever he's always surprised. One day I'll win the Nobel Prize just so he'll drop dead of shock.

The big thing that happens this Christmas is that, as I set the table for Christmas dinner in the evening, I say it's odd that I've not had a card or anything from Aunty Nelly. I sent her some Newberry Fruits and the postage was horrendous. I say to Dad 'Has anyone heard from her?' and sometimes you just know something's wrong but you don't know why. Dad clears his throat and says 'No. We won't be hearing from Nelly.' And my belly plunges and I want to go to the loo and I can't breathe and I say 'She's dead?' But Dad says no, she's fine. I don't understand. Mum comes in with a jug of water and says 'Your father's told you all you need to know.'

We eat dinner in silence, roast turkey and thirty different vegetables and millions of sauces, and little sausages like cremated toes, and then Mum jumps up saying in her bright voice 'Oh! Crackers!' When she comes back with three gold and red crackers

I can't bear it any longer. I say 'I want to go to Golborne to see her.' And Mum snorts, and says something like 'I want doesn't get, Miss' but I can't really hear because suddenly I'm trying not to cry and my heart hurts, missing Aunty Nelly so much. It's ages since I cried and my throat is sore with the effort of it all, and even my shoulders ache. A great fat tear lands on my plate and melts into the gravy, and then another, and I'm all hunched up and snotty and my tears in the gravy look like a marbled book cover and Mum says 'Wonderful! Happy Christmas!' and Dad sighs, and I get up and go upstairs. No one calls me back.

What with buying the Christmas presents, I've only got one and sixpence in my money box so I take it and find a pencil and my rough book from school and put my coat on, and my school scarf, and my outdoor shoes. My hands are trembling but I don't know why. Dad comes to the hall and watches me. Mum comes to stand behind him and she takes a breath to say something but he gives her a look, a look he never gives her, hard and like a warning, and she bites her lip and goes back into the dining room. He asks where I'm going but I can't speak, and he says 'There aren't any buses on Christmas Day.' I manage to say I don't need a bus. He says, and it's like it's the first time he's ever seen me, really seen me, a person, 'You miss your Aunty Nelly?' And I'm so shocked I can't think of anything to say. It's only taken him four years. I want to say 'What do you bloody well think, you eed-jit?' But I don't. I just walk out. It doesn't feel like I'm fourteen. It feels like I'm forty. Or thirty. Or twenty-three.

Directory enquiries takes ages to answer and they take ages to find the Legh Arms, but then they do and I write the number down. When I make the call I explain that I haven't got enough cash to wait but it's Shirley who answers and she understands and she says she'll run and get Nelly and I'm to call back in five minutes.

So I sit at a bus stop imagining five minutes, and then I go back into the phone box. And Aunty Nelly answers and she's crying and I'm crying and we can't understand each other and we're laughing and after a bit we can talk properly and I have to put in more money and we wait while it clunks down and then she calls me her little love and that sets me off again and then there's the pips and she shouts 'Give me your number, give me your number!' So I do. And when the line goes dead I put the phone back in its rest and wait. When the phone rings I snatch it up and we're tumbling over each other with questions – she wants to know am I well and am I happy and I say yes and yes, and then she says 'You're not, love' and I say no, but it doesn't matter now and I ask how Kitty Lob is and she says Kitty Lob is the bane of her life and it's time she was bloody put down and that makes me laugh again because she's been saying that for always. She says she sent me a cardigan she knitted in yellow double knitting wool from the market but Norah sent it back and said it was too small. I never saw it and Nelly says 'I know, lovey, I know.' She tells me she wrote to Daddy and said she was worried about me because she hadn't heard from me, and then, after a lot of letters backwards and forwards, it turns out Mum hasn't been posting my letters. Although I put stamps on them and everything. She has to tell me twice because I can't make sense of it but then I do and she says 'Your Dad was so cross with her, and he's so mortified but she's his wife now and......'

I say 'I know.' I understand. I say it's alright.

Aunty Nelly's been writing to me, too, but I never got any of them. I can smell Aunty Nelly, I can smell her and see her and although she's in the pub, at the bar where the phone is, and I'm in a phone box that smells like the boy's loo in Warminster, I can see her so clearly in her back room, by the fire, with Kitty Lob on the hearth and the washing drying from the ceiling and the rag rug. And we just smile at each other down the phone, for ages. And then we agree I'll call every month, and she'll accept reversed charges and she'll make it right with Shirley. The first Sunday of every month. We run out of things to say, so she asks if we went to Midnight Mass and I say no, Dad said we've done it once and there's no need to make a bloody ritual of everything. Just before she goes I say 'Aunty Nelly?' And she says 'Yes?' And I say 'Did my Mammy love me?' And she says 'Oh, Lucy, love, never doubt that. You must never ever doubt that. What a question.' So she didn't actually say it. She didn't actually say that Mammy loved me. Just that I mustn't ever doubt it. Another way of saying 'You must never ask it.' So I won't.

When I get back, they're watching the telly, some variety show I think. I look in the sideboard in the dining room, which is verboten, and there they are, Aunty Nelly's New Berry Fruits. The door to the sitting room's closed so I just go to bed. This Christmas thing, I could do without it.

Maybe I am not the sort of person you can love. Maybe that's it. Maybe Aunty Nelly loves me because I'm her sister's girl, not because I'm me. Because Mum finds it hard to, and so does Dad now, and Uncle Alf didn't. So, maybe I'm not. But Aunty Nelly cried and that must mean something.

WAXING SENTIMENTAL

Martin's home and he's tall and his hair has gone blondish in the sun. Dad is very pleased to see him and Mum is trying hard to smile. I feel sorry for her now, more than anything, because she can't be happy. Even when we're sad, most people can't help seeing the funny side of things but she can only manage an uncomfortable sort of quick smile. I wish I could make it better for her. Martin says she has no sense of humour. I think maybe I have too much, and that's just as bad because you can get into trouble with it, like last week when the head mistress farted and I said 'No more curried eggs for you!' like *The Goon Show* and she turned around and glared at us all and the whole hall was in hysterics. There was this little flicker in BX's eyes, and I think she was a little bit hurt, so I felt sorry. I wished I'd just shut up. Miss Baker took me to one side afterwards and said I wasn't ten years old any more and there's a time to leave childish things behind. And something about being the class clown. I sort of know she's right but I love making people laugh, the smell of the crowd and the roar of the grease paint. Joking. But I'm sorry I made everyone laugh at BX.

Martin says I've grown and I say 'both ways' and he says no, just upwards. I tell him that I'm a fat sort of person and he says Mum should get her eyes tested. Funny how he knew it was Mum's words, but then, she tells everyone. Even in the shoe shop she told the lady that I wear my shoes down being so fat, and in the Home and Colonial when she was buying New Zealand butter because she got used to it over there, she says to the man behind the counter 'Not that some of us' and then she rolls her eyes at me 'need any more fat at all.' I pretend I haven't heard.

Martin's brought a carved box for me and a whole roll of kingfisher blue silk for Mum and a Kukri, which is a curved knife, for Dad. He's put it up on the wall so that if we ever get burglars it'll be at hand. And then Martin says he got me something from duty free, because he came back on a civilian flight. It's wrapped in gold paper with a bow, and we all look at it for ages, and then I open it. It's a watch, not a Timex , a proper adult watch, Avia. It's beautiful, silver and mother of pearl. I love it.

Poor Martin.

Every single afternoon, he buys a return ticket and catches the train to Bath, so he's waiting at the gates by Bath Pavilion and we walk to the station together and he sits with us on the train. I don't think there's ever been such a good brother as him, even if I do only see him once a year. He takes me and Mary to Maynard's Sweet shop and we can buy anything we want, but we don't tell Mum.

In the evening we play Scrabble while Mum and Dad watch TV in the other room. He's got a whole month off but he's going to spend a week with Aunty Nelly and then he's going to try to find Peter, because he's vanished off the face of the Earth and the Navy won't tell Martin where he's gone. He says he has to, because he promised our Mammy that he'd look after Peter but if he'd known what an awkward bugger he was going to be, he'd have kept his fat mouth shut.

Martin takes us all out to a Chinese Restaurant which I've never been to before. I don't think I've ever been to any restaurant, so I wear my Avia watch. It's all very nice, with velvet on the walls and paper lanterns and a candle on the table, and I say 'Can we light it and wax sentimental?' And everyone laughs and laughs (Mum smiles) and I realise it was a pun and I pretend it was on purpose. But it wasn't.

Martin starts talking to the waiter in a foreign language and the waiter looks at him like he's mad. Martin must see that the waiter doesn't know what he's going on about but he keeps on talking. The waiter looks at Dad and Dad says 'The bloke's Chinese, Martin, not Malayan.' And the waiter says 'I'm from Derby.' but Martin has another go. We start laughing but I wish he'd shut up now. Enough's enough. Everyone's looking.

Martin wants everyone to be happy so he keeps telling us to order the most expensive things but I just want the special fried rice which sounds lovely. Martin keeps telling us to have the duck which is nearly five pounds. It's like in Maynard's Sweet Shop when Mary and me want milk gums and he wants to buy a box of chocolates for two pounds. He hasn't realised that making people happy doesn't work like that. I don't know how it does work but it doesn't work like that.

When Mammy died Martin decided that he had to make up for it for everyone. When Mammy died Peter decided that he had to make everyone pay for it. But me, I think that when people die there's no making up for it, and no revenge, no point in any of that. The world doesn't even notice. God doesn't blink an eye. Yes, He does. I know He does. Shut up.

The food is lovely and Martin orders banana fritters for pudding and when Mum says 'Not for Lucy' he goes very still and looks at Dad and Dad looks away and then Martin points at me and says to the waiter 'Banana fritters and ice cream' and Mum doesn't say anything. They are lovely. Just unspeakably lovely. I told Beth about it on Monday and she says she's had them lots of

times and I'm right, they are the best pudding the world has ever
known.

Martin and me go for a walk the day before he has to go back
and Martin talks about Mammy and about me when I was little
and it's lovely. He says that when *Listen With Mother* came on the
radio and they said 'Are you sitting comfortably?' I would shout
'No! No! Wait for me' and run from wherever I was and climb
onto Mammy's lap and we'd listen together, like you're
supposed to. And he says that in Egypt when the dew sparkled on
the dusty ground in the morning, I thought the droplets were
fairies and I'm so happy because I remember that too, and I
remember my swing, and the old shepherdess who used to lift up
her yashmak to waggle her loose brown teeth at us. And he tells
me about my best friend Barry, who was an officer's son, and how
we decided we were going to marry one day. I remember Barry
suddenly, so clearly! A little blonde boy with a big wide forehead,
and I remember going to tea at his house and feeding his Alsatian
under the table with crusts because his Mum said no ice cream
unless we ate all the sandwiches. I remember! My brain clicks
into some sort of working gear and I remember. I thought I'd
forgotten everything and it's like a small miracle. Martin says it's
all there, and it'll come back, bit by bit. I'm so happy. I feel like
it's the best gift ever. And he has two little photographs of Mammy
in his wallet and I look at them and look at them and look at them.

When he goes to put them away I ask if I can just hold them
and he lets me, all the way home.

We talk a lot but there's a question I'm desperate to ask and
it's a question I daren't. I want to say 'Did Mammy love me?' But
I don't want to hear the answer in case she didn't very much. I
daren't ask because the answer might be what Peter said – that
she loved him, not us. Or what Aunty Nelly said 'Never ask that'.

So I don't. There's a bit of me that knows for certain she did love me, but I would just love to hear someone say it. But I can't risk it. I know that if Dr Kildare was there, and he was looking at me with his sad eyes, I would risk it because he would know to say the right thing, but this is Martin and he's lovely, but he thinks that a box of chocolates will make you happy, so God knows what he'd come out with.

When we get home Martin asks Dad where the family photos are and he brings out an album that Mum's made and Martin says, no, from before Mam died and Dad looks unhappy but he goes upstairs and comes down with two albums. Martin says 'Lucy's going to choose a few photos and we're going to make a book for her' and Dad says OK. We go out to the corner shop and buy a scrap book and now I have Mammy in bed, and Mammy on the beach with Aunty Betty and they're both in knickers and bras in the sea, and Mammy holding me up to the sky, and one of me crying because Martin was taking a photo and walking away from me to get the picture right and I thought he was leaving me in the middle of a field. You can see the Nissen Huts where we lived and Martin says 'That one was ours.' I don't remember any of them, but as I look at them and we stick them in the book, I think maybe I could grow the memory with time.

And then he's gone. British Guiana. Dad says he'll come back speaking Zulu to Scousers and we smile because we both love Martin.

NIL CARBORUNDUM

O-Levels next year. If you're in 4X you choose between Greek and Latin and Maths. The clever stuff. If you're in 4Y you choose Science or Physics or Chemistry. The quite clever stuff. If you're in 4W you can plump out your exams with Needlework, Cookery and Art. The idiot's choice, Dad says.

The cookery teacher is a local councillor with delusions of grandeur. We have to make Swiss Roll and call it Roulade and Beef Pies and call them Steak Wellington. Mum says it's costing a fortune and every time I say 'I have to have..' and tell them what I need, Dad hits the roof and shouts about the bloody money that's being wasted on me. It's no good trying to explain that I don't even want to do cookery, because that just makes it worse and he says I'll do what I'm bloody well told and silk purses out of sow's ears and then Mum says again, again and again, that he'll have a stroke. One day, she says, I'll kill my father. Which would be ironic as she would be my first choice.

Fishface is our needlework teacher but she doesn't know a French seam from a French letter. We had a sex lesson last week so we're au fait with it all now. In the First Form it took everyone else one term to sew themselves an apron for cookery. Three years later, I've still not finished mine. The head mistress said there's an excuse for my maths, because I don't have the brain, but there's no excuse for the apron because any idiot can sew. Fishface looked a bit put out but she didn't say anything.

Homework can take hours every night, but I don't mind. I sit in the dining room with my head right next to my tranny and I listen to radio Luxembourg. As soon as I finish I have to go to bed so most nights I pretend I've not finished so I can stay up till nine and then Mum opens the door six inches and says 'Bed time, beauty sleep.' Two whole words that aren't absolutely necessary, the effort that must take!

I wish I could stop calling her Mum without it causing ructions. But it would.

I love homework. I love English. We have to write an essay every weekend but sometimes I do two or three and I hand them all in and Mrs Ash marks them all. I got a nine and three quarters last month for an essay about 'A Night Out'. I wrote about a party in a night club with models and pop stars and champagne and music. Mrs Ash said I should have written about something I knew about but she said it was very persuasive anyway and gave me the highest mark she's ever given! Ever. She must be the best teacher anyone ever had, and we love her. Well, I do. Beth and Nicky don't. She said if anyone uses infer instead of imply, she'll murder us with some degree of pleasure and that no one would blame her. When she says these things we know she's joking but her eyes pop a little bit and her cheeks go red. Anyway, I don't care. I love her.

And I love Radio Luxembourg. Sometimes it whistles and whines so I fiddle the knobs and get the American Forces Radio which isn't as good but I do like the voices and I want to go to Texas one day, and New York, and Detroit City. They play a lot of The Everly Brothers and Bobby Vinton but we're all a bit mad about The Beatles, and Beth brought in a magazine about them. My Beatle is John and hers is Paul, even though he's a bit girlish, and Nicky loves George. Some people say he's thick but I say no, he's saturnine. And they all go 'Ooooh, get you!'. Everyone says I sound like John but I can't see how, because I'm not from Liverpool although Golborne isn't that far away and when I was queuing up for dinner I somehow ended up telling a load of Second Formers that I'm his cousin and now half the school believes it. I'm going to save my daily sixpence – which Mum gives me with this closed face, and no smile, like it's hurting her – for a Beatles fan club magazine. I keep thinking Mum's going to get tired of giving me a sixpence every day and just give me half crown once a week, but no such luck. So every day she sighs and roots around in her purse, although we both know she gets five sixpences from the paper shop every Saturday, and she always always makes it seem like I'm robbing her and Dad. 'No one else gets sixpence a day, I'll bet', she says and in my head I say 'No, most of them get ten shillings a week.' But I don't say it out loud.

John Lennon is beautiful. He's like a Greek God and Mrs Ash said that there's nothing wrong with appreciating male beauty as long as we don't go overboard. I realise now that Clint Walker and Cliff Richard were just crushes, because what I feel for John is much deeper, more mature. I think it's a sort of sexy thing. I told Aunty Nelly on the telephone, but I left out the sexy word, and she said she doesn't blame me, he's a good strong lad and he's nice to his Aunty. I said that if I ever get to go out with him we'll go up to Lancashire and take both our Aunties out to tea and she knew it was a joke but said, dead serious, she'll wear her new hat. All Aunty Nelly's hats are the same, but she gets a new one every year, at Easter. Grey, felt, shaped like the top of her head, and just big enough to tuck her bun in.

On Monday we're in the new Science Lab in Saint Anne's building and we're supposed to be revising for the exams, so we're all talking and Beth is showing us how to draw a perfect circle without a compass, and Der Fuhrer has gone out to collect some Latin homework from 5X when I see them. If you look out from Saint Anne's you look over the garden and then the old netball court where Beth broke my nose, and then Bath Pavilion, where they have shows and plays and Christmas markets. I'm watching clouds and trying to make things out of them, when a van pulls up at the back of the Pavilion. And then I think maybe my daydream's going a bit far because there's three men and they look like, but they can't be, but then I screw my eyes up and concentrate and I'm sure they are. I look around but Beth is in the middle of everyone doing her circles so I nudge Nicky and whisper and she looks and she sees them too and we grab our books and we exit, pursued by bear, down the back steps so we won't meet Der Fuhrer on her way back in. We don't even think what we'll say when she sees we've gone. We run and try not to clatter because the back stairs go past all the other classrooms.

I start to run across the garden but Nicky grabs me and hisses 'They'll see!' so we keep to the hedge and the path and when we get to the netball court we crouch down like the Austrian resistance running from Gessler in William Tell and I realise that this is real, this is actually happening, this isn't just in my head. And I can't help laughing out loud.

When we get to the garden between the Pavilion and the new netball courts, we're safe if we keep to the end where no one will be able to see us among the bushes. We scramble up by the wall and there they are. The real live Beatles. John is sitting on the back of the van, smoking a fag, and Paul is talking to him, his back to us, fiddling with something. We call and Paul turns and John squints at us, the smoke in his eyes. He's gorgeous. He says 'Bloody hell, it's Saint Trinians.' And Paul laughs and comes over, but he has to scramble up the stones because the Pavilion is lower than our wall and we're up high to them. John stands and gives him a little shove up and then Paul turns and gives John his hand and he pulls him up, and there we are, talking to actual boys. Men. Actual pop singers. John says 'Alright, girls?' And at first I can't say anything but then I do, and I don't know what I say but they both laugh and Ringo wanders out of the Pavilion and Paul says 'Hey, come and see what we've found at the bottom of the garden' and John says 'Fairies' and they laugh and John winks at me. He winks at me! Ringo scrambles up and says something's broken, a bracket, and he hasn't got a spare but John and Paul don't seem very interested. I say I come from Golborne and John sings 'I'm a lassie from Lanca-shire' and we all laugh some more and I tell him about Aunty Nelly having tea with his Aunty Cynthia and he thinks this is hilarious. I don't know why. I tell him that my Aunty looked after me when my Mammy died and he says his Mum died a couple of years ago, but his Aunty brought him up too.

George comes out and jumps on the van and carries something into the pavilion but he doesn't look at us. He seems fed up. I feel sorry for Nicky because he's her favourite. Ringo asks if he should walk into town and see if he can find a music shop to get a new bracket and Paul says 'Up to you.' But I think maybe there's been a bit of a row because only John and Paul are properly chatty and looking at each other like friends. Ringo shrugs and sort of clumsily slides back down the raised bit and goes into the Pavilion. John sits on the wall and then Paul does, too and we sit between them and John says 'Fag break.' So we sit there until John's finished his cigarette and then they jump down and I say to John 'Is it right you've got a baby?' And he says ' Two months now.' I think he must be a lovely Dad so I say so and he pulls a face and says he doesn't know about Dads and I say neither do I.

The lesson bell goes and Nicky says 'We've got to go' and she runs off, waving and Paul does this funny two handed wave and sort of screams 'Bye bye, bye bye' like she did. I think maybe he's making fun of her. A bit cruel. She looks sad and goes pink and shouts 'Come on, Luce, RE.' But I let her go. Paul wanders off and John says 'Not going to RE?'

Then, just when I think he's going to follow Paul and unload the van with George, who's crashing cymbals and telling Paul he's not his Dad so shut up for fuck's sake, John changes his mind, takes out another fag and lights up, leaning against the wall. He says 'What's this step mother like then? Wicked?' And I say no, but she's not very.... He laughs and says 'She's not very?' and I don't know why but I tell him, I say it, out loud, 'I'm not someone you can love. She's tried and tried. Dad says give it time, but we've given it years now, nearly five, and she just doesn't.' He doesn't say anything and I think I've ruined it. I think I've properly ruined it and now that he knows I'm not someone you can love, he'll notice my quarter to three feet and my stupid bum and I'll see it in his eyes and I'll feel worse than I did when I met him first off. Why did I tell him, when I've never told anyone before?

He looks at his cigarette and twirls it, then picks a shred of tobacco off his lip, 'Your name's Luce?' I nod, 'Thing is, Luce, it's the same for everyone. The most important things to do in the world are to get something to eat, something to drink and somebody to love you. That's what we're all trying to do. Find that one person.' And it's really quiet. I say 'I thought it might be you.' He doesn't smile, he says 'You never know. Maybe it is. When you're all grown up, come and find me, and we'll see what happens.' I know he's joking but it's a kind and serious joke, not a cruel one like Paul's two handed wave. So I say 'Thank you' and he says 'No problem.' I think I should shut up now, before I ruin it all for proper, but I can't help it, I say 'What if I'm thoroughly unloveable?' And he blinks, a funny short sighted blink like Fish-face when she cleans her glasses, and then he says 'You're not.' Which is an odd thing to say because he doesn't know me and it's an odd way he says it, fierce and muffled. I don't want to go but I have to, so I start to turn away and he scrambles back towards the Pavilion, down the rocks and the little raised bit, and I turn for a last look and he calls back, cheerful, 'Hey, Luce, I'll be waiting. Until then, nil carborundum illegitimi.' And he winks. And then he's gone.

The funny thing is, now that something really nice has happened, and I've actually met an actual pop singer, I don't want to tell anyone. It's my secret, mine and his. I swear Nicky to secrecy but she didn't really like Paul and she was disappointed with George so she says we can just tell everyone we went to the biology lab to learn the dog-fish diagram.

EVERYONE IS DEAD

Aunty Nelly's dead. I can't say anything else about it because I don't know. Dad came out to the shed on Saturday morning when I was getting the stuff together for another damn day of weeding, with a letter in his hand. He was really sad, no pretending for once. I don't know what to say. I don't know what to write. I just stared at him. I can't go to the funeral, because it's too far and I've got school and I can't stay overnight because... because because because. I ask if she'll be buried near my Mammy and Dad swallows and says he doesn't know.

So we know fuck all about fuck all. Aunty Nelly. My Mammy's sister.

Down, down, down
 into the darkness of the grave
Gently they go,

It's stuck in my brain, over and over.

The Beatles are on the TV and in magazines and on the radio and everywhere. Everyone loves them, apart from Dad and the nuns. I don't want to be the little boy who cried 'Wolf!' but I know that's what will happen – along with being Max Bygrave's best friend and with Winston Churchill being my godfather, and Val Doonican being the choir master in our church in Omagh and Fancy Smith in *Z-Cars* being my Uncle, they'll just go 'Oh, that

Lucy Gannon, she's at it again' and then I'll get upset and all the magic will go.

But Aunty Nelly's dead.

Nil carborundum illegitimi. And I won't.

I didn't tell anyone at school but Dad must have phoned because at Assembly we prayed for her soul. It's a funny bloody God who has to be persuaded and coaxed and bribed to be kind to a nice woman like my Aunty Nelly. And you shouldn't call God funny. Or bloody. But it's right, isn't it? Why would a just God let someone off just because someone prayed for them, but torture someone else for years just because they didn't have anyone who loved them enough to pray for them? I ask Him that but there's no answer. This God thing, I'm sure we've got it wrong.

I haven't cried for Aunty Nelly. She should have the whole bloody world crying for her but I haven't managed even one solitary tear.

On Friday Mrs Ash gave out the marked essays and mine was the very last. She's just about to hand it to me and she stops and she says 'I've broken the practice of a lifetime. For thirty years I've taught English and I've never given ten out of ten.' And then she plumps the essay down on my desk and I have it! I have ten out of ten! She ruffled my hair like I was a dog and everyone crowded round and she said there was a terrible misunderstanding about the semicolon, and she'd given up on the 'ands' but nevertheless. She asked if I'd like to read it out and I said 'No, thank you' and everyone groaned. Mrs Ash said it was my prerogative and should be respected. We must always remember that writing is about writing, not about applause. The essay was entitled 'My Hero'

My Hero By Lucy Gannon 4W

The world is full of heroes; They might be aquiline Greek heroes, with statues dedicated to them, muscled men hefting a discus or a javelin. They might be the square jawed cow boy riding into Laramie to face his enemy, outnumbered and outgunned. They might be the mild mannered hospital doctor, quietly saving lives on a daily basis. Or they might be ordinary people, who look just like you and me, who will never have a statue raised to them or a book written about them, unlikely heroes whose heroism is never known, let alone celebrated. So, how do I choose one, as this essay demands? I thought about it for five minutes, give or take four minutes, but then my fingers were itching for my Conway Stewart and the smell of ink and the scratch-ratch of the nib on the paper and I could wait no more.

I have chosen an unlikely hero and a very nervous man. He has blotchy skin between his fingers and he pulls the skin around his nails until it bleeds. When he's nervous he talks to you with his eyes closed and sways. He isn't very good at preaching but he climbs the steps to the pulpit every Sunday and he faces a sea of faces, like Shakespeare's sea of troubles, and closes his eyes and begins. He has a mother with stones in her gall bladder and a Canon who calls him 'the boy' but he saved me from Purgatory when I thought no one ever could.

And then I went on about praying for my Mammy and how she was supposed to be in Purgatory for forty years, but Father Sullivan explained that was all so much old rubbish and how I could sleep afterwards and how even the dreams about my Mammy's grave have stopped now. Anyway, I didn't think it was as good as my nightclub essay but Mrs Ash did.

I was going to tell Dad about my perfect essay but he went straight in to listen to the news and then when Mum called me through to do the washing up, we just passed in the hall and he was busy talking about some new rule at the County Court so I just smiled at him and Mum closed the door on me, as per. So, I never did tell him.

When I'd done the washing up, Dad went into the sitting room and Mum brought their plates through and said she'd do them, so I could get on with my homework. Anything to get me out of her sight and that's OK by me.

I was drawing a card to send to Aunty Nelly's funeral when Radio Luxembourg started to whistle so I fiddled around until I got the American Forces station. It wasn't very good, and I had to have it on so low that I could barely hear it, but it was better than nothing. I'd finished the card and was putting it in an envelope when there was this break in the music and a really panicky voice. Panicky but serious. I turned it up a tiny bit.

If I hadn't been in such a state, I would have remembered to keep my mouth shut, but I didn't. I went straight into the sitting room, without even knocking, and Dad looked up and Mum jumped like someone had poked her, and scowled but I didn't apologise or anything, I just came straight out with it. 'They've shot the President.' Dad stared at me. I said 'They've shot John Kennedy. I just heard.' Dad sighed and I realised he thought I was making it up. I knew I was in for it then, but it was too late to turn back. 'On my radio. The American Forces station. They've just announced it.'

So now the wicked stepmother's confiscated my tranny. Bugger. I had to go straight to bed where I prayed that the doctors would save him and that everything would be alright.

Prayers don't work. He's dead. JFK is dead. Everyone is fucking dead. We said prayers at Mass, and no one can really believe it. I kneel there thinking 'I knew before any of them' but it doesn't really matter, because he'll be dead for ever. There's no medals for being first with that news.

As I walk out, behind Mum and Dad, Father Sullivan's tidying up the wax droppings around the BVM statue and I remember his one bar electric fire and his unfinished crossword and the cake with the cream that was off and I start to cry. I cry and cry and cry with the sadness of everything. Dad mutters 'Bloody hell' but he puts his arm around me and it's lovely. Then he gets embarrassed and takes it away again, quickly. I can't stop crying. Everyone thinks it's about JFK but Dad shakes his head at them and mouths 'Her Aunty' and Father Sullivan says we should sit down in a pew till everyone's gone, so we do. Mum and Dad go to get the car, and Father Sullivan says 'Tell me, then.' And I say 'I was crying for you, Father.' And he looks a bit surprised and then he says 'There are better things to cry for, trust me.' And I say 'You've only got the one bar on a terrible dusty little fire.' And you can see he's trying not to laugh and I get angry because I'm not really crying for the bloody one bar fire or the cake with the cream that's gone off, and he should know that. Him of all people. And then he stops smiling and he says 'It's a bugger, Lucy, all of it, and there's no understanding it. You cry all you like, why not.' And that makes it sort of OK, so I stop crying and blow my nose and Dad comes in and takes me home.

On Monday the nuns are in a terrible state. They've all been crying and some of them keep swallowing hard and being all steely and full of 'God works in strange ways' and 'He's gone to a better place'. Like that makes it somehow better. It bloody doesn't. It's his funeral today and Beth and me sneaked into the back of the boarder's sitting room to watch the news. His little boy was there, looking serious and tragic, wearing a coat with a velvet collar like the ones Prince Charles used to wear. We're to have a special Benediction for the repose of the President's soul, and there's going to be a Mass on Wednesday. We're sending a letter to his widow and his little children. It's very sad. I don't want to think about how sad it is. A thousand bloody 'ands'. I'll never get the hang of it.

The death of a hero. I write an essay about it when I get home but I keep crying and the ink runs and I can't see properly, so I give up and go to bed. Fuck it.

THE LITTLE PRINCE

If this was a filum, with Danny Kaye for example, it would be A Good Sign. But this is real life and the happy-ever-after ending isn't in sight yet, so I'm not holding my breath. But I suppose it is a glimmer of something. Mum and Dad went to Corsham on Saturday and came back with a puppy. He's a nine week old Shih-Tzu, his name is Wong, and he's a little smasher. I can't believe anything could be so pretty and so gentle. He's bloody lovely.

He's not house trained yet so for now he's confined to the kitchen, which means I can see him only when I go in to do the washing up, or walk through to go to the shed to clean the shoes. Mum says it's crucial that he gets into a routine, but so far she hasn't produced a to-do list for him. Once she's taught him to read, though, she'll be sticking it up next to his basket. Leaving me in there with him, while they have their dinner, is nearly killing her. She's convinced I'll pick him up, or drop him or, I don't know, eat him or something. It agitates her to see me stroking him and him responding to me. I think maybe she knows that her dislike of me is getting out of hand.

We've got two books on the breed, and photos of adult dogs with long hair, flowing down and over the ground, and mini pony tails, on their foreheads. They look a bit soppy but Dad's as besotted with the photographs as she is. He's read up on them and they're called Lion Dogs and they were owned by all the emperors of China. Pekingese dogs used to sleep in the big billowing arms of kimonos as sort of living muffs but Shih-Tzus are too big for that, so they were companion dogs.

When I go in to do the washing up Mum dithers in the doorway, sort of quietly agitated. I know she wants to say 'Don't talk to Wong' but even she knows that would be totally potty so instead she says things like 'He's just been fed so he needs to sleep.' Or 'Don't disrupt his training.' Anything she can think of to keep me from getting any sort of affection from a ten week old puppy. Tragic. Talking to me at all is difficult for her, so she looks at Wong as she says it, and he thinks she's talking to him so he bounds out of his basket on his fat little Queen Anne legs and she bridles and sighs as if it's my fault, and shoves him back in. I know that the dog is partly an Anthony substitute and partly a distraction from her hatred for me and partly something Mum and Dad can fuss over together. Poor little sod. And here's him, thinking he's just a puppy.

Wong has one abiding sin. He adores the marigolds bordering the boring lawn in the boring garden. If you look at him from behind he looks like he's being sick, but he's just shoving them down his gullet as fast as he can. On Saturday I was weeding the borders (how I hate this place) and I could see him working his way steadily through the marigolds. I didn't stop him because in Orchard Crescent you have to take your pleasures where you can. After a few minutes Mum rapped on the window shouting 'Wong! No!' and Wong turned around, startled, and there were two orange flowers, unmistakable, one each side of his little smiling mouth. As Mum abandoned the window and flew out of the back door, still shouting 'No! Wong! No!' as if it was the most heinous crime anyone could commit, he gave one great big heaving gulp and they both vanished. Mum turned on me 'Couldn't you see what he was doing?' I said 'Sorry, I thought I'd better not interfere with his training.' She just glared at me, swept him up and flounced back into the house, saying 'Mummy's very cross with you, Wongy.' Apparently marigolds are poisonous. If she's his Mummy, poison would be the merciful option.

Watching Mum and Dad with the dog is fascinating. I find myself thinking about Anthony more and more, and what life would have been like if he'd lived. There are so many ways it might have gone. Maybe Norah would have found it easier to be with me, and with another son maybe Dad wouldn't miss Martin and Peter so much, because I know he does. And maybe he'd relax a bit more about me being so thick, because Anthony would make up for it. And maybe Anthony, who would have been starting nursery school just about now, would have noisy little friends and bring laughter and happiness and life into the house. Maybe.

I think that if I was clever I would study psychology. Or psychiatry. Either that or I'd be a forensic pathologist, living with death and dead people and finding out what killed them. Or I'd be an undertaker. I like the thought of washing a person when she's dead, or he, doing the last thing for them that anyone on this earth will do, and talking to them quietly, gently, so that if they're still there and they're frightened they'll know they're not alone yet. It's horrible being alone. But you have to have Maths for all these things. Not for just washing bodies, though, so maybe it's a possible. I thought I might like to be a nurse but Mum said you need Maths for that, too, or you'd be killing a diabetic every five minutes. I said 'A different one every five minutes, or the same one over and over?' and she looked at Dad and he said 'Don't try to be a smart alec. It doesn't suit you.'

Last year, in English, we read 'The Odour Of Chrysanthemums' by D.H. Lawrence and it reminded me of Aunty Nelly's back room, and Uncle Alf's coal dust when he came home from the pit, and it was all about washing a dead miner's body. Well, it was about more than that, it was about all sorts. No one else in the class knows what it's like to live in a mining village and when I told them that it's so real, and it's right, everything that's in the story is absolutely right, Mrs Ash looked at me in her 'Ahah!' way, as if she could see something in me that she hadn't seen before, so I shut up. If it had been a sentimental story I think I would have cried, but it wasn't sentimental, it was real, and so I didn't. That night I had the Uncle Alf dream.

I've taken eight O-levels and when we get the results I have to choose two A-levels, but without Maths or Science, I can't go to University. I'd quite like to teach English but even if you want to teach PE like Beth, you have to have Maths. She's lucky because she's going to get her O-level so the world will be her oyster, but it's funny that I can't teach anything at all although the only thing I won't have is Maths. And Latin and French. And I dropped Chemistry and Physics. And I'm probably going to fail Geography. Maybe it's not that funny after all.

There must be something I can do, though, so it's just a case of finding out what.

When I leave school, I would quite like to live on my own, with absolutely no one else in the whole house, in a white room, with no furniture and no cupboards or anything, so that I never got in the way of anyone, or even of the light, and didn't even have a shadow. I would come home from my job as a kennel maid, and I would sit on the floor, against the wall, and I wouldn't be in anyone's way and I wouldn't have to step sideways and apologise. How dramatic. How tragic. But then, after about two minutes, I'd say 'Sod this' and get up and go into another room, full of records and books and posters of John Lennon and great tumbling piles of flower power clothes like bell bottoms and ponchos and white boots with Chelsea heels. And I'd put bells on my fingers and bells on my toes and light a fag and twist and shout my way into the Cavern (my flat will be just around the corner) to hang around with all the lads. Fabulous. That's my plan. I think I'd like to be a boozer. I'd like to get drunk on Saturday night and stay drunk till Monday morning. Someone called Brendan Behan used to do that but he died a few months ago and Dad said good job, and if it hadn't been the booze it would have been an Army bullet between the eyes. When Dad hates someone he really hates them. But the serious bit, the bit I really want, is the living alone bit. In a house where there's no one else and you don't have to worry about getting in the way in the hall, or crossing on the stairs or being so loathsome you can't risk anyone seeing you. That would be fab. No one to worry about. And the Beatles around the corner.

Anyway, I asked Mrs Ash about Brendan Behan. She said he was an Irish writer, plays and stuff, so it seems a bit harsh to execute the poor bugger. Then there was someone on the radio saying that he was wise in his own way, and a real wit, and they remembered how he said simple but truthful things, like "The most important things to do in the world are to get something to eat, something to drink and somebody to love you." and I remembered John and felt a bit sad that it wasn't his thought after all, but just borrowed.

Wong's hair is growing really fast and Mum's going to get a spinning wheel to make things out of it. It makes me feel a bit sick, thinking of a cardigan or something made out of dog hair. Imagine the smell when it rains. But they've joined a Shih-tzu club, and apparently everyone's at it. She grooms him for nearly an hour every morning, even though he's only a puppy and his hair's only half grown – God knows how long she'll do it for when he's got proper flowing tresses like in the photos. She puts talcum powder on him and brushes it through, over and over, then she puts his top knot into a plume, and trims the hair between his toes, and wipes his bum (!) and then she even cleans his teeth. I keep thinking of Mary's Mum saying 'She needs something to fill her days, that one' and I think that's what poor Wong is. Along with everything else. A little bewildered prince, like the poor Dalai Lama, when he's just a baby, taken away from his home and the way of life he should be living, and turned into a little god, whether he wants it or not. The object of adoration and veneration. And then I think of Anthony and wonder.....

BELONGING

In December I'll be seventeen. I got a job at the Harris Sausage Factory in Calne for the summer holidays and I love it. I love the bus in the mornings, the air thick with fag smoke and hair spray, and the girls, and the noise. I love the boys, looking at us sideways. I love the girls in the back seat back-combing each other's hair and trying to paint Dusty Springfield eyes, protesting every time we hit a pot hole or the driver brakes. I love leaving home at half six and not getting back until seven at night. I love the pay packet, even though it all goes to Mum apart from two pounds. I don't want to be a convent schoolgirl, I want to be a factory worker. Dad says that if my exam results are no good, that's exactly what I'll be. Good. I hope they're terrible. Dad's in a foul mood because Wong's taken against him, and he's got a bandage around his thumb where he was bitten, and a scratch on his other hand where Wong tried to latch on but Dad shook him free. Mum gathered Wong up and told Dad it was his fault for pestering him and Dad said, quite mildly considering 'Bloody hell, Norah, I just stroked him.' The grooming takes an hour every morning now and she gives him a quick tidy-up after every walk and he's never out of her sight, except for Mass when he waits in the car on a specially made crochet blanket. The Dalai Lama is not the happy little bouncing thing he used to be.

So it's great being out of the house all day. Normally I hate the holidays but I bloody love this summer. My friend at the factory is Pam, a thin girl with big teeth and a way of walking like a boy, and she's only a year older than me but she's engaged to Alan who's moved in with her and her parents. They must do it because they both sleep in a double bed which only just fits in Pam's room. They live on a farm, in a cottage, because her Dad is a cowman and the house goes with the job.

We went up to her Mum's for tea and it was beans on toast and vegetables, which I've never had before, not beans *and* vegetables, but Pam said they eat what's in season in the garden and if it's tomatoes you have bloody tomatoes with your custard. I said 'But only in custard season, when the custard bushes are heavy with the stuff' and her Dad looked at me from under his eyebrows but he didn't say anything. Sometimes I say daft things and don't stop myself in time.

Pam's Mum has gall stones and, because I don't have anything else to say, I say I know someone else with them but when Pam's Mum asks me about this person I have to say I haven't actually met her. And Pam's boy friend, Alan, says 'Acshewally.' and I try not to mind but then I just make it worse by saying that it's Father Sullivan's mother. Alan hoots and makes the sign of the cross and does what he thinks is a genuflection and I should be embarrassed but Pam winks at me and I'm not. Pam and me, we don't care. We just laugh and laugh. Everyone's afraid of Pam, except me, because she's fierce and angry a lot of the time. I just like her. She thinks I'm odd but she doesn't care either. We're an odd couple and that just makes it even more special. Alan starts to sing a mock hymn and she tells him to shut his stupid face and he goes 'Oooh, pardon me, vicar.' But he wanders off so that's OK. I'm not that fond of Alan.

The house is tiny and packed with stuff, the kitchen is so crammed you can hardly move, and it's all shabby and old and it smells of cooking. It's absolutely lovely. It reminds me of Mary. Pam's Mum keeps burping, which she says is the gall stones, and her Dad says 'And that's not all she does'. It's as if they're all stark naked and they don't care. Nothing to hide, no covering up, they don't even think before they speak. I suddenly think about the Garden Of Eden, before Adam and Eve realised they were naked, and I think 'This is it, this is Paradise.' There's no room for anyone but there's room for everyone.

I've even told Pam about John Lennon. It was tea break and we were in the stairwell, so she could have a fag. She didn't laugh or say I was mad, she just listened and then nodded. I told her I'd not told anyone else and she looked at me, right in the eye and said 'I'm honoured.' which isn't the sort of thing she says usually.

Alan has a car and he drove me home, with Pam twisted around in the front seat, talking all the way. She shouts a bit but that's because of the noise in the factory and she says if I stay there I'll be the same. I don't mind. I'd give anything to work at the sausage factory. I know everyone there, all their names, and we shout at each other silently above the noise and make faces, like we're a bit mad, and it reminds me of elocution lessons, so I open my eyes wide and en-un-ci-ate but I don't make any sound at all, and old Peggy, on the other side of the links room, doing a special run of M&S chipolatas, knows exactly what I've said and gives me a big thumbs up. Then I do:

And how can man die better Than facing fearful odds, For the ashes of his fathers, And the temples of his gods?

and Peggy stands there trying to make sense of it, while the pork links pile up on the conveyor belt behind her. So I do it again, with mad gestures and now everyone's looking and it's funny. Then she gets the joke and does a cheerful V sign at me and mouths 'You're bloody bonkers.' And we laugh.

I love Harris's. There's a lad called Paul and he looks a bit teddy boyish, which is quite old fashioned , but he's smashing. He calls me the schoolkid, but he winks. I think he might want to kiss me and, just in case, I'm getting through two tubes of Polo mints a day.

When I got back on Thursday, there was an envelope on the hall table, and it was open, but it was addressed to me so I knew what it was – my O-level results. Dad and Mum were watching TV, with the door closed. I changed my shoes and picked it up. I didn't know whether to take it upstairs or read it there. I thought it must be bad, just lying there, opened, and the TV on, and the door closed. And then Dad was there, not her, just him. He stood in the doorway and I could hear Cliff Michelmore behind him, and he said 'What a waste of bloody time and effort that was.' I felt terrible, with tears in my eyes and as I unfolded the paper I was waiting for him to hit me, ready for the shock of it but it didn't come. Breathing was a bit hard. It took a minute to see, to focus on the words, but I blinked and took a breath and made myself read it. I'd passed them all. I didn't know what to do, what to say. Dad said, turning away 'Get out of my bloody sight. I can't bear to look at you.' None of it made any sense to me at all. I said 'I've passed them. Every single one of them.' Dad turned back, the door to the sitting room open now, and we stared at each other. Someone had to say something so I said 'Grade One English, English, History, Biology, Art. Grade Two everything else.' And Norah came to the door and stood next to him, welded to his side, and I saw her hand slip into his as he said 'Grade One's a fail, you eedjit.' I started to laugh, nerves and something else, a bit like anger, and I said 'No, Grade One's the best pass. Grade Six to

Nine are fails.' He'd got it the wrong way round. And he said 'Are you sure?' But I didn't answer, I just grabbed my bag and I didn't even change my indoor shoes again, I just sort of stumbled out of the front door, and I let it slam and it was like a big fat exclamation mark, that slam. And I ran all the way to the phone box to call Beth and she's passed all hers too, but without so many Grade One's although she did get Maths, which makes it even better because we can be happy for each other.

I went for a walk because my head was going wild, one minute really happy about the exams and the next wishing they'd all been fails so I could go to the sausage factory and the next thinking about how pleased Mrs Ash would be that I got two Grade 1's for English and how I might go on to get my A-levels and surprise Dad for once and for all.

When I came back, Mum had been round to Mr Jay who's a teacher and he'd told her I was right. Dad was a bit embarrassed and Mum kissed me, but she's out of practice and so am I so we bumped our foreheads and it was cringey. Dad said we'll need to talk about the future but Mum said maybe I'd like to have a bath first because I smelled of sausage meat.

I had a bath and washed my hair even though the water was only lukewarm. Mum and Dad were in the front room with three glasses of sherry. I knew they were waiting for me but I felt that I should, maybe, still knock on the door before going in. It was momentous but I didn't know why. Yet. I had my hand up, my knuckles turned ready to.... But it felt odd so I didn't. I took a breath and went in.

Dad gave me my glass and then raised his, 'Here's to Lucy, who's surprised us all.' I don't know why he's so surprised, I've had the De Brabant prize for four years running, the prize for the hardest working pupil in the form. Four years running and he's surprised! And last parent's evening Mrs Ash told him I was a gifted child. If a teenager can be a child. He has a great propensity for surprise. That made me think of Jane Austen and I must have smiled because Dad winked.

Mum smiled a thin smile, and she was quite stiff and jerky, with an angry mottled colour, so I knew something was coming. Dad said there's no rush, and I must take my time considering all the options, but they're both agreed that everyone will be happiest if I start to make my own way in the world. At first my breath was taken away, and I couldn't quite make sense of it. And then I did. Dad said 'And it's what you want, too, isn't it?' I didn't have an answer so I just nodded. He nodded back, relieved.

I sipped the sherry, and then I asked, how long do I have? And Baron Hardup looked even more uncomfortable and said that they both agree, leaning heavily on 'both', that I should make my plans by Christmas and aim to put them into practice in January. I can carry on at school until then, because it's no good hanging around the house, and the teachers can maybe give me some pointers anyway. I said 'Harris's?' And Dad said no, it wouldn't look good. I said I don't mind, I love it there and Dad said no, quite harsh, and he looked very unhappy, so that I felt really sorry for him. All his brothers and sisters are teachers, and he's spent the last six years going on and on about the convent education he's giving me, so a sausage maker wouldn't be easy to explain away. Mum put her two penny worth in and said it would be a sin to waste a good education, after all the sacrifices they've made. No one says anything else and we just sit there. Then I make the mistake of putting my hand out towards Wong and he goes for me. Bloody little bastard.

QUO VADIS

I've only got another week at the factory so I went in the next day, Saturday, and did four hours overtime. I can't remember much about it. Pam wasn't there because her and Alan are at some market in Somerset, selling her Mum's chickens. I just felt cold. Ever since Dad told me about leaving home, I've felt cold. I couldn't bear to look at them, and they couldn't bring themselves to look at me, either. The next day, Sunday, was the most excruciating experience of my life. I'd rather have the day I nicked the ten shillings, and the day after Mammy died both rolled into one than live through that again.

After Mass, I went to my room to be out of the way and my pay packet was on my bed. So, that must mean I can keep a whole week's wages and I suppose I'll be able to keep next week's too, with three days holiday pay. I counted it all up and I could be starting off with seventeen pounds in my spotted handkerchief, tied onto a stick, as I make my merry way through the world, whistling a happy tune. I was putting it away in my school purse when Dad knocked on the door. On second thoughts, he said, it would be best if I didn't say anything about all this to anyone at the convent, until I've decided where I'm going and what I'm doing. It's none of their business, apparently.

The next day they drove into Corsham, and I knew something was brewing and I had a quiet dread, a nameless wordless quiet dread. Let's call it, for want of a better word, fear. I realise now that I'm afraid all the time. From the moment I wake up to the moment I go to sleep. Afraid that Norah will say something, or Dad will deliver another piece of startling news, and that something unexpected will rear up to grab me by my fat neck and shake me. That I will have to live like this for ever. In dread. I don't know what it's about.

They came back with another puppy. His name is Sultan. School started again the next week, and I was glad that I couldn't tell anyone what had been decided, because I didn't know how to say it without sounding like Orphan Annie. I didn't want to see their pity, to hear their soft voices saying soft daft things that don't help. Beth kept asking what was wrong but after a bit she stopped, I think she knew that whatever it was, it was too big to talk about. I felt strange, listening to my friends and thinking 'They're children.' I feel so old now. Alone.

On Tuesday we had to choose our A-levels so I put down English and RE and I felt awful when Mrs Ash stopped me in the corridor to say I was her prize pupil and she'd have to go a long way to find another like me. She said she wished she taught A-level but she knew I'd do well in the Fifth Form. It was on the tip of my tongue but if I told her the truth all hell would have broken loose and I'd have to see BX and there'd be letters to Dad and ructions. I'd end up crying and nothing would change. They don't want me. That's the bottom line. No, not quite. The bottom line is that when my Mammy died, I should have died too. They should have killed me at her funeral, like suttee. When your mother dies you lose your place in the world and that's all there is to it.

It feels like everything's different, I'm different, and everyone should just take one look at me and know. But they don't. I can't sort it out what I'm feeling, I feel really bewildered that I'm leaving so soon, and all that suttee stuff is sad, but it's not that simple. I'm excited too, and a bit confused, and just completely strange. At dinner time yesterday I realised that it's not just a secret but it's also a lie, to act as if everything's normal when it isn't. And I try to imagine what Beth will feel like if the first she knows about it is when I don't turn up for the new term after Christmas. We went into the basilica and there, sitting under the PE kits and whispering, I told her everything and she cried a bit, but I kept saying 'It'll be OK, it'll be fine.' I really do think that. I do. I don't know how but somehow I really do think that everything will work out in the end. And it's so dull, being sad. So exhausting being frightened.

It rained and we had indoor rec and I jumped up on the stage and did 'Not fade away' like Mick Jagger, all pouty and bum sticky outey, and everyone cheered. The whole school cheered and I felt weird, angry and happy and victorious. Madam Celine said I was shameless and I said, out of nowhere, without even thinking about it or knowing if it's true, 'No, just defiant.' And she said 'You'll never be a prefect at this rate.' I looked at her sweet ignorant Irish face, and I laughed and laughed and laughed so much I began to feel a bit tearful.

Anyway, anyway, I'm ready to go. Now I know how much they really don't want me, I can't wait to go. I've always known, but now I can't pretend that I don't. They don't pretend any more and that frees me. There is no fairy at the bottom of the garden, however much I want to believe there is. I am unloved and unlovable. The really strange thing is that it's not me that's in the way any more, but Mum. She stays in the kitchen as much as she can, and when she does come in she sort of hurries, flustered, and she's awkward with Dad and Dad's a bit awkward with her. And they're really quiet. Like they're both ashamed or something. Maybe they are, a bit.

I haven't got any homework because we're not in our new classes until all the exam options are sorted. For the first time ever, I think, what the hell, and I go into the front room and sit in front of the TV. Dad looks up from his paper but doesn't say anything. So, holding my breath, I put the TV on. I actually lean over and turn the TV on and it's *Top Of The Pops!* I've never seen it before so I watch it, still not properly breathing, waiting for Mum to come in and create ructions, but she doesn't and it's fab. Dad doesn't say a word.

I can't sleep and the nights seem to drag on for ever. I used to do the journey to Golborne in my head, the walk to the station, the train to London, the walk through crowded streets, weaving through the red buses, another train to Wigan, a smaller one to Golborne, the walk to Legh Street. The last step was a magic leap through the air into Aunty Nelly's lovely fat arms. There's no Aunty Nelly at the end of that journey any more, so now I do another one, a journey in time, starting the night Mammy came up and kissed me and was miraculously cured. The next morning Peter isn't crying when I wake up, and Aunty Polly's making a bacon sandwich, and Mammy's sitting up asking for a cup of tea and she's wearing her blue cardigan, and so the journey goes on and on, all the way to now, when I'm sixteen. It's lovely. The way it should have been.

In the way it should have been, Peter didn't leave home, and Martin didn't sign on again after his National Service, so there we are, two brothers and a sister and their parents. A Mam and a Dad and not a single fucking Shih-Tzu in sight. Imagine. Just imagine. What if. I'd be heading to University, where I would study Theology and English Literature, thin and tall and gorgeous like Twiggy. That's taking it a step too far. This picture pops into my head, of my Mammy looking at the thin me, dumbstruck, saying to Dad 'Eeh, what's happened to our Lucy?'

Then I think about the life Norah would have had if she'd never met Dad, and I give her gingivitis and all her teeth fall out. Hah! But it makes me feel spiteful and I can't work out the Anthony thing, would it have been good or bad if he hadn't been born? Mrs Ash says metaphors always fail in the end so you shouldn't beat the life out of them trying to make them work. I think that, like metaphors, 'what ifs' always fail in the end. We're stuck with how it is.

The weeks drag past but I still don't know what I'm going to do or where I'm going to go. I look in the back of the Daily Telegraph but they all want managers and executives. I think I might be able to get a job as a chamber maid in a hotel, but I don't know what to do about that. I think I might be going a bit mad. I feel a bit mad. Solitary and wordless and mad. I can't keep a hold of a single thought for more than a single second. Or less. I want to talk to someone about it but there isn't anyone. I can't go to Father Sullivan, I just can't, and anyway he's being sent to another Parish so he has enough to worry about, what with his Mum and everything. And I don't want to write to Martin in Borneo because there's nothing he can do and he gets upset when he thinks of me here in this house, and Peter's God knows where. So there's just me. Me and Christ crucified, still up there on that damned cross above my bed. I'm not even in a fit state to pray. Not so much a state of grace as aggrieved, exasperated, angry, peeved, narked, fed up. I could get a job working on a Thesaurus. And that makes me laugh. Thing is, what I sort of know deep down but keep forgetting, is nil carborundum illegitimi. I could get it tattooed on my bum, or somewhere I can see it.

So, arse. Life goes on.

After school I went to Benediction, which is still my favourite time of all, and when the oldest nuns came in, the retired ones who potter around all day getting lost and smiling, and drinking tea as pale as custard, I looked at them and something clicked.

On Wednesday morning I had a free lesson, being a Fifth Former now, and I went along to BX's study and knocked on the door. I can't say she was thrilled. She kept saying 'Are you sure, Lucy? Are you absolutely sure?' And I just nodded my head and said 'Yes, Madam, I want to be a nun.'

HIGHGATE, WITH COMRADE MARX

I went to the Novitiate for the weekend. I heard Mum telling Dad that if I have a vocation they mustn't stand in my way, but Dad said nothing. He trained to be a priest but he backed out when the war came so maybe he's got mixed feelings about me following his confused path. Beth thinks I'm mad, and her Mum says that I've been pushed into it and it's a disgrace. I know she's right but I don't want her to be, I want to protect my Dad even now. I think of what he said years ago about the youngest son and the ugly girls being sent off to the church and I think he was right, we *are* savages.

I feel so alone it's a sort of delirium. And there's something else growing and I can't push it down and it's just pushing at my chest and rising in my throat and I think it's anger. No, I don't think, I know. When we went to Mass last week, Father Sullivan came over and of course no one said anything about the convent or me leaving school. He asked me how school was and before I could say anything at all Dad said, quickly, to shut me up, 'And how are you, Father?' And I suddenly felt this great black boiling rage. I don't know where it came from. I wanted to shout 'My father's thrown me out and I'm going to be a fucking nun' to see the shock on Norah's face as Dad slumped to the ground, clutching his chest, but of course I didn't.

And then, as they burbled on about the weather and the garden, without even thinking about it, I did the next best thing, I said 'I'm glad Brendan Behan had a Requiem Mass, Father.' I don't know where it came from or why I said it, but it was pure genius. Even now he's dead, Dad can't bear to hear his name without doing a sort of snarl. Dad turned on me, incredulous, as if he'd been slapped in the belly with a wet fish, there outside the Church, with all the little First Holy Communion girls running around in their white dresses and all the boys in bow ties. Father Sullivan was smiling vaguely, trying to work out who, what and why, so I filled in the gaps 'The writer, his funeral, I saw it on the news'. I can't remember exactly what Dad said next but it involved the bloody church and the murdering bastard IRA. People started looking and Norah writhed in embarrassment. Father Sullivan, who must have felt like he'd just been ambushed by two lunatics, took a step back and said, bewildered and mild, that the Mass is for sinners as much as for saints, and I said, loud and clear, heavy Irish like Behan, 'The most important things to do in the world are to get something to eat, something to drink and somebody to love you.' 'Now half the bloody church was looking. It was sort of out of the blue, what Mrs Ash would say was a non sequitur. Something else was needed so I ploughed on, desperately reckless now, ready to be hanged for a sheep and a lamb and whatever other piece of farm life came to hand, 'What the hell difference does it make, left or right? There were good men lost on both sides.' Dad met my eyes and I just stared back at him. I stared back at him! He said, dead soft 'Is that another quote?' And I said 'I believe so. He also said they sentenced him to death in his absence so they could execute him in his absence, which was a good joke, don't you think?' It was all I could do not to say it in broad unapologetic Ulster brogue. The silence was ugly, jagged, solid. It went on for ever, Dad was just itching to give me a damn good slap and I wanted him to, so I could punch his stupid face in. Several times. And then Norah linked his arm and did a whinnying laugh and pulled him away. Father Sullivan looked at me, puzzled, and I grinned and shrugged. They got in the car and drove off and I was glad. I walked back, let myself in, straight up the stairs, and lay on my bed, grinning like a demented something or other. Completely thrilled. Strange.

I couldn't give a toss about Behan. I think he was a drunken oaf with the occasional clever phrase thrown in, but it felt wonderful. Grown up? Oh, yes. Bloody marvellous. The next day Norah stayed in bed with a migraine, Dad couldn't look at me, and I walked to the egg farm and took all day about it.

The next weekend was my visit to Highgate Convent, to see if it's the place for me. It was lovely there. You could hear the traffic, just over the wall, on Highgate Hill, but inside it was tranquil, almost silent. Just the distant hum of buses and lorries reminding you of how lucky you were to be in here and not out there. Marx lay under a stone slab somewhere nearby.

I had a lovely little room, overlooking the gardens, and a Bible and a prayer book and a prie deux. It made me think of all the paintings and Mass cards of Theresa of Avila and I wondered, just briefly, if I could ever aspire to sainthood, if I lived long enough. The room wasn't lilac. Haha.

I arrived on Saturday and we said the Rosary before lunch and after that, recreation. I was put with a novice, Claire, who's nineteen and from Galway. I told her that my family were from Mayo way back but she said that she's never been out of Galway, except for coming here. She was very nice but hadn't got a lot to say for herself so we did a jigsaw which she said has three pieces missing. She didn't know how many times she'd done it, but she guessed probably five or six. She said it with a soft smile. I think of Aunty

Nelly calling Joe Grimshaw a soft lad, and I hope that if ever she falls through a tin roof, she'll find a soft landing.

After that it was more prayers in the chapel and then tea which was bread and butter and jam and apples. The butter was margarine. A lifetime of margarine. That made me wonder about the whole idea, right enough. While we ate, one of the nuns read the Bible, the book of Obadiah, which sounds like a name from *Round the Horne*, and I thought of Gruntfuttock, our favourite bit, and felt a pang of homesickness for Beth, not for home. Bethsickness.

We were all in bed by seven, but we were up at five and down to the chapel again, for Mass. The priest was ancient and Claire whispered to me that he's been retired thirty years already. Mass took hours, you couldn't hear a word of it, and when he lifted up the Host a nun had to put her hand under his elbow. Breakfast was horrible porridge and tea, and then we had Fellowship, which is prayer but in the sitting room. I know that if I told Beth about it, she'd say it was dire. But it wasn't. It was lovely. We all belonged there. I don't know how else to put it.

After prayer we sat and had Community, which is talking. The nuns asked about my family and somehow I couldn't lie to them, so I started at the very beginning, knowing that when I got to the bit where when Mammy died that would make all the questions melt away in a flood of Irish sentiment. It did, of course. 'God bless the child' and 'Rest her soul' and all that, looking at me with such pity that I felt a terrible fraud. I said 'It's alright, I don't mind' but that made it seem like Mammy was no more to me than a bus driver or a shop lady. Or I was a cheerful psychotic. I felt my cheeks burning so I went to an old blind nun who was trying to unravel a skein of wool and getting in a right state. If people would just not talk to me, everything would be fine. I didn't mention Uncle Alf.

After cabbage and bacon I had an interview with the Head of the Novitiate, a French woman, not just an Irish girl with pretensions. I was all ready to answer her if she asked about God, or my faith. I'd rehearsed saying 'Like Thomas, I have my doubts, but like the father of the possessed boy, I pray that God will help my unbelief.' which seemed pretty good to me, if I do say so myself, and wide enough to cover a multitude of sins (literally) but she didn't talk about God at all, or even about the order. She was more interested in my Needlework and Cookery O-levels. I think maybe they're a bit short of those skills in Highgate Convent, and the breakfast was pretty rough right enough. I wanted to ask her if I could serve at the altar during Benediction but she was finished with the housekeeping skills and onto my periods. My periods! I only started them last year, the last one in the class, and beginning to panic that they'd never come and I'd be like a prehistoric reptile, hermaphrodite. I'm not used to them yet, let alone talking about them to a nun! She said 'Are you pure?' I made a joke of it and said 'Purely sinful, I am that.' because her being French somehow made me want to be more Irish. I nearly broke into 'Begorrah' and 'by Jaysus' but I just stopped myself in time. Then she rang a bell and another older nun came in and Frenchie gave her the nod, a meaningful sort of nod, and she took me down to the garden and we sat there chatting for ages and it was lovely. She said 'See how all the squirrels are playing around us?' And they were. And she said 'See the lovely gardens.' And I did. Then she said 'It's beautiful weather today, is it not?' And I said it was. Then she took my fat hand and she put it between her boney ones and she said 'Sometimes it rains, and it's cold, and miserable. And there are forty-eight women locked up in that house behind us, and they're all trying hard not to kill each other.' I wasn't sure if she was joking. I got this picture of Mrs Murdstone and I looked up at the windows on the top floor but of course there weren't any shadows, no one darting back out sight, no pale face pressed against the glass. She patted my hand and said 'However bad life is, Lucy, this is not the place of refuge you're looking for.'

Rejected by the church. Well, not quite. They've said I can come to the Novitiate for a few months to try it out, but they've made it clear that they don't think I'm suited. And the thought of the unending rain and the monstrous regiment of murderous women has persuaded me. And the margarine. Two days was just right. Sixty years would be pushing it. So, what now? I still fancy working with Pam but when I phoned her she said I'd never afford a bedsit on a starter's wage, and that, said Luce, is that.

I bought two thousand piece jigsaws and sent them to Highgate to Claire but when I posted them off, I felt sad, and wondered if I've made the right decision. Not the jigsaws, the vocation. I had a letter from Martin saying don't do it, Lucy love, do not do it, so Dad must have told him about the convent. He'd underscored the words and said he'd go AWOL and come home and drag me away if he had to. I wrote back, by return, to say false alarm.

Bugger. Now what? In a week it'll be my birthday and no one wants a seventeen year old. You can't go to teacher training college or nursing school till you're eighteen and anyway, I haven't got bloody Maths, have I? So much for considering my options. I wish Aunty Nelly was alive. I could sleep in the parlour where Mammy died, and get a job at the peanut butter factory, or the pub. But she isn't. They're all keeling over like skittles.

Bugger bugger bugger. There must be somewhere I can go. Bloody Borstal or somewhere. See? There are so many options, I'm spoilt for choice.

Exactly two weeks after my seventeenth birthday, 16th December 1965, instead of catching the train to Bath, I cross the bridge to the London platform and, in my convent uniform with my homework under my arm, I catch the train to Swindon. And in Swindon I am welcomed with open arms and they throw flowers at my feet and pile my arms high with money and chocolates and promises. Crackerjack!

When I come home I tell Dad that I've joined the Army and he says 'It'll make a man of you.'

GUILDFORD

So far, The Women's Royal Army Corps is a bit like the sausage factory but with quite a lot of lesbians. I thought they'd all smoke pipes and dress like men and it turns out they're just like the rest of us, apart from two sergeants who sound like blokes and one corporal who does an amazing tiger purr/roar.

My number is 427991 and I'm in a four bedded room with Heather, Chrissy and Jennifer. It's so fabulous I can barely think, or speak or write, or stand upright without laughing. I've come home. The Army is my family and I've missed it without even realising.

Our uniforms are a bit unimpressive, and the stockings are grim, but we're all going into Guildford the first chance we get to stock up on American Tan tights. And the bras! You have to put them out for kit inspection but no one wears them. They're like two ice cream cones on a strap. Heather says they're the Army's answer to Russia's guided missiles.

We started marching the very first day and it was the funniest thing since Gerry Battersby's milk siphon. Berry (the purring lezzer) said we were the worst intake she's ever had. Next week we have to learn about Venereal Disease, and when Heather told me what that was I didn't know where to look. What would Fish-face say? Well, not a lot, she'd be too busy being carried out on a stretcher. We've had lessons in shoe cleaning – like I need that! I've grown up watching Dad and Martin bulling their boots so

I've been showing everyone and Jenny's the ironing queen so we're all getting help from her, creating precise pleats in skirts and knife sharp creases on every shirt sleeve. We laugh the whole time, even when we're polishing the floor (they call it 'bumping') or cleaning the lavatories. I'm so happy I can hardly take a breath. It's Harris's multiplied by twenty.

This is the best thing that's ever happened to me. At NAAFI break I did my Mick Jagger impression and the whole place stopped to watch and afterwards they cheered. What a laugh.

We had to go to the Education Block and take some tests and then last week we had to talk to a sergeant about the results. He said that I have a very high IQ which made me laugh out loud, but he said the tests don't lie (I bet they do) and that I had the highest score he's seen. Because I don't have any languages and no Maths it cuts down the options but I could choose between the Royal Signals or the Military Police. I've read all the bumph and I knew the Signals meant Maths so I told him I'll be a redcap. Martin's going to be chuffed because when he did his National Service that's what he was, before he signed on again and went into the Infantry. When she saw the list of all the specialities we're going to, Berry said 'Bugger me! Red cap, no drawers' and got really arsey. Turns out it's against military law to be a lesbian so they don't like the Military Police much. Heather's going into catering, which is what she wanted, Jenny's going to train as a driver, and it looks like Chrissy's going home because she won't stop crying and she's rubbish at just about everything. I can't believe I'm not subnormal after all.

I've brought my tranny and we have it on all the time. Every morning we have a room inspection and all our kit has to be perfect and on display, and the place has to be shining so bright it would blind you. We were just finishing the final touches when the look-out shouted that the Duty Officer was on the ground floor and making her way up, so there was the usual flurry and panic and everything got slammed, shut, put away, windows closed, everyone standing to attention. Then, just as we heard the foot-steps in the corridor, I realised that the Beatles were still singing 'Michelle'. I'd closed the tranny in my wardrobe. We stared at each other, standing there, at attention, appalled. I could see our hopes for Guildford C&A, and chips on the way back, melting away. The Duty Officer and her entourage came in and there was a tiny, miniscule frozen moment, and then she carried on like she couldn't hear anything at all. It would all have been fine, but Michelle ended and some idiot DJ started burbling, pitched so high it would waken the dead, warbling and crowing. The fool. You could see the NCOs were struggling. And then, just as Captain whose-yer-face picked up Heather's shoes, Nancy Sinatra started with 'These Boots Are Made For Walking' and that did it. We all collapsed. The Captain walked out, shaking her head. As Berry marched out, past me, she rolled her eyes and did a tiny purr. Five minutes later someone yelled 'OK ladies, NAAFI break. Back in thirty.' and we couldn't believe we'd got away with it, but we had. Good old Berry. I'm never going to arrest her for being a lezzer now. As far as I'm concerned, she can do whatever it is lezzers do all day long, on the parade ground, stark naked and blowing a bugle.

I've no idea what they do. I don't want to think about it too much but you can't help wondering. Heather says Berry fancies me, but she comes from the Outer Hebrides and washes her hair in Daz so what the hell does she know about anything? Her hair's thick and wiry and very long. She puts it up in a weird bun and says she'll never cut it because men are mad for a woman's hair. She's small and square and she walks like a camel and her accent's so thick you have to run through what she's just said in your head before you can make any sense of it at all. So never mind men being mad for a woman's hair, they'd have to be mad, full stop. But she's fab. A right laugh. When I did my Mick Jagger she followed it up with 'Ferry Across The Mersey' and you could just about tell what the song was but no one could work out who was supposed to be singing it, best guess was Alvin and the Chipmunks.

We do our basic training here and then I'll go on to Chichester for military police training. We can invite people to come and watch our passing out parade in our last week here. I'd have liked to ask Martin or Father Sullivan but one's still in some jungle and the other's been sent to Glasgow, so I thought I wouldn't have anyone and I was quite happy about that. Then I had a letter from Dad asking about the parade so I had to tell him. I thought they wouldn't come because I told them you can't bring dogs (which could be true, who knows?) but Dad wrote back to say that Wong and Sultan will be happy enough in the car for a couple of hours. Bugger. They're only coming so he can tell everyone how well I'm doing and how happy I look, and pretend that I didn't want to stay on at school. Which, as it turns out, isn't far from the truth.

I've had a couple of letters from Beth and I sent great wild screeds back but she's going on about pocket money and double History and it feels like all that was eons ago, in another world, another life. Irrelevant, just as my great screeds will be irrelevant to her. By the time she finishes college I'll be twenty-two. Well, so will she, but I'll be quelling riots in some theatre of war, wearing my Brigadier's uniform and she'll still be living at home. Time to move on. That's Army life for you. Dad used to say 'Never get a pet, you'll only have to leave it behind one day.' The same applies to friends. And family, as it turns out.

I've had three letters from Martin and one from Dad, who says my room's been turned into a guest room. We had to fill in a form to say where we'll spend our leave at the end of basic training. I looked at the question for a long time and it was like something was holding my wrist. I just couldn't write the words 'Orchard Crescent.' I'm not even sure Norah would let me in. I asked Berry if I had to take leave and she said yes, but I could spend it here in barracks. So, that's alright.

I lay in bed last night and it hit me, really hit me; I never have to go back. Never. It was like something magical, my eyes pricked, and my skin tingled and my bed started shaking and I couldn't help it. I couldn't stop. I didn't want to. Heather groaned 'For Gawd's sake, girl, shut the fuck up.' And Jenny said if I didn't stop laughing she'd shove the iron so far down my throat my shit would come out pleated. Fab.

POST SCRIPT 8TH
DECEMBER 1980

Louise came through at seven this morning, but she may have been up and about long before that. She wakes up happy, sunny side up, and she plays in her room quietly until she hears one of us in the bathroom and only then does she make her presence known. She bustles through to us, full of some dream she's had or some important thing she has to tell us. Yesterday it was something about an elephant's trunk, but neither of us could understand what the story was and she trailed away, exasperated that we weren't enthralled by her words, stubbornly refusing to explain any more. Today the message was clearer, she wants to go on the top deck of the bus so she'll be able to look over the wall of the graveyard again. She's three. What's the great attraction of a graveyard?

I'm pouring tea when George comes down, in his grey jacket and a paler grey shirt with a silver tie and he looks just a bit gorgeous, and I tell him that and then can't stop myself explaining that gorgeous means many coloured, that he's my peacock. He drinks his tea and pulls a face at Lou. Scots, quiet, undemonstrative, an engineer, a cross between Steve McQueen and John Mills. My blast from the past. I'm in love with all the heroes of my childhood rolled into one. He lets me love him, and although he seems quietly amused by the idea, we rub along OK.

There's nothing special about today. Not yet.

Lou's already in her little armchair, with blue rabbit and a bowl of Weetabix when I turn the radio on. I can hear George backing the car onto the road, and I go to the window to give him a wave before he engages first gear and swings away. I think it must be the first item on the news because as I raise my hand, I hear it. John Lennon was shot, late last night, New York time. While we were sleeping, he died. I don't know how long I stand there, my hand raised.

The watcher at his pulse took fright. No one believed. They listened to his heart. Little – less – nothing! – and that ended it. No more to build on there. And they, since they were not the one dead, turned to their affairs.

I see him clearly. John. He looks at his cigarette, picks a shred of tobacco off his lip, 'The most important things to do in the world are to get something to eat, something to drink and somebody to love you. Find that one person.'

It's really quiet. I say aloud to the grey window pane, 'I thought it might be you.'

It's the end of something, but it doesn't have a name, this thing that's ended, Aunty Nelly stroking my hair, trying not to cry, Mammy dying like Nelson, Anthony on a satin pillow with a love-stitched forget-me-not, Father Sullivan with his one bar fire and a crossword half-done, Eleanor Rigby and Father McKenzie, wiping the dirt from his hands as he walks from the grave, a silent house where Cheyenne Bodie waits for me in a lilac room. Done.

I think of the kind boy who didn't know about dads, the almost wise things he said, and the many foolish ones, the ones he borrowed and the ones he sang, and the man he grew into, a smug guru, posing in a bed in the Hilton Hotel while the whole world laughed at him and at the woman who loved him. I think of the girl who left the convent and joined the Army and battered around the world, ricocheting from one disaster to the next, writing to him for years, and of all the signed photographs that came in reply, churned out automatically. I wonder where they are now, all those black and white photos, all those strong jawed young men, strutting with a guitar, or pensive, owlish, boyish, some lost and sad, the later ones bearded, shaggy, sandalled, pale, myopic, like a picture book Jesus.

And the word, the name, grabs me. It socks me, shakes me, head to toe. I left Christ behind a long time ago, happy to step away from the Belsen figure on the crucifix and the pious pink cheeked man of the Mass card, so why am I so suddenly and brokenly touched by the thought of him? How have all the wild strands of my life come together at this moment, in the shadow of this God? If this is a prayer, then it's not for John, and not for me, but for all the sadness and lovelessness and emptiness of the whole damn world. A world good enough and bad enough to die for. Which, I suppose, is the whole point of the story, every story.

And in that moment, I understand it all. A brief moment of completeness. In that moment, Jesus reaches down, like that terrible old film in Ulster a lifetime ago, Jesus reaches down, comes down, and the cross is empty and the story is told.

When I turn around, Louise has wandered away, her lips moving silently as she tells her story to some unseen companion. She pushes a naked, raddled Barbie into the compost of the spider plant and I look at the tiny detritus of a morning in my life: Weetabix scabs drying on a child's bowl, uneaten toast, his mug, my tea now cold, a half dressed doll with a drawing on its belly, last night's curry plates and a sheet of paper with an engineer's careful handwriting. I pick it up. 'How to change a wheel.' Not that again.

My cheeks are cold and tight and I think I must have been crying. Why is it so bloody vital that I know how to change a wheel? When the world is full of sorrow, young men dead, mothers gone for ever, the loveless and the lost, why must he write his careful, engineer's instructions, explaining yet again that nuts should be loosened alternately. Like something John might say in a John song. Your nuts should be loosened alternately, i.e. every other nut. Your nuts should be placed in the hub cap so you don't lose them. Your nuts should be tightened up again evenly and alternately, i.e. every other nut.

Why does George insist that the one thing I must understand, in a universe of unanswered questions and rage, is how to change a wheel?

Maybe he can't bear to think of me and Lou, stranded, at the side of some road, in the cold and rain, without him. Maybe this is his love letter to both of us.

Nil carborundum illegitimi, John.

ACKNOWLEDGEMENTS

As I've written this book, I've remembered so many people whose kindness ran through my childhood like a golden thread: the priest who walked me home after my botched die-from-the-cold attempt, the nuns who didn't call me a thief when I was one, Mary Ash who broke her rule to give me ten out of ten for an essay, and Mary Knight and her parents, who showed me what a family could be. I no longer know any of these people, and most of them will be dead, but I thank them across time.

I am also very grateful to people who are still alive and kicking, and without whom this story would not have reached the publisher:

Thank you, Rob Filgate, who was first to read it, the first to understand my need to write it, and the first to encourage me.

Thank you, Anne Cakebread, who turned into an unofficial literary agent and nagged and coaxed and bullied me into submitting it to Seren.

Thank you, Mick at Seren, for putting up with wild capitals and irrational punctuation.

But most pressing of all, my thanks go to the God who loved me when I thought I was loveless, and who loves me still, and for ever.

All I have and all I am, is his.

AUTHOR NOTE

Lucy Gannon is the author of 8 plays and 18 tv dramas or series, including *The Best of Men*, *Soldier Soldier*, *Peak Practice*, *Bramwell*, and *Dad*. She won the Richard Burton Award for New Playwrights and has been writer in residence at the Royal Shakespeare Company. She has also won a Bafta Cymru for Best Screenwriter, a Prix Europa, the WGGB Award for Best Radio Drama among many other prizes, and was awarded an MBE for services to television drama.

She is currently developing scripts and mentoring writers for BBC Wales, and contemplating other writing projects. She lives on the coast, in the far west of Ceredigion.